Sprouting Spiritual Growth

— a Memoir and Guide to Spiritual Journaling —

MARIE HIGGINS

Print ISBN: 978-1-54390-217-4
eBook ISBN: 978-1-54390-218-1

Publisher: Bookbaby

Requests for permission can be sent to:

Marie Higgins

cardinaltouch@verizon.net

DEDICATION

To those who have encouraged my creative side:

Mom, who enrolled us in art classes all over the city

Mrs. Hummel, my 7th & 8th grade teacher

Mr. Ron Hof, one of my high school English teachers

The Abington Art Center and its many teachers

*Grandma Ryan who wanted a copy of my speech after
her 60th wedding anniversary celebration*

*My husband and children who enrich and inspire
me by using their own creative talents*

God, the greatest Creator of all

TABLE OF CONTENTS

SIGNS OF THE TIME

Trees dusted white
And still standing.
Winds blow gently outside.
Blazing blue-red flames in the fireplace
Slice through cut wood
From felled tree in our backyard.
I sit alone.

Community children visit rarely anymore.
Houses sit empty during the week.
Neighbor's garages release them in the morning
And swallow them up on their return.

I long for childhood days,
In and out of neighbor's homes.
A fireman's family on our left,
Policemen homes on our right and over the alley.
Across the street the milkman's daughter was my best friend.

FOREWORD

I am an avid reader and I have enjoyed being in book clubs to discuss the writing, what we can relate to, what we find puzzling and what we have learned.

In one of these book clubs we primarily read books of fiction and many of them were on best seller's lists. A problem arose because many of the books were about extreme trauma and they impacted me deeply. It wasn't because I had experienced similar traumas. It was because these books surfaced feelings that I didn't want to feel. So I quit that book club and I joined a club which discussed non-fiction books. The discussions are factually based and generally don't require me to consider my feelings.

Don't get me wrong, I do think feeling is important. Fortunately, I found another outlet for expressing my feelings. It was something new to me. It was called spiritual direction and the simplest definition I can give it is this: it is a way for individuals to aid others with developing a more intimate, personal relationship with God.

Over the course of several years with a Spiritual Director, I learned different ways to pray which allowed me to sense and experience God's will for me. Some of the methods included walking meditation, and praying with a variety of objects including clay and pictures. You'll find how-to instructions in the back for a few of the disciplines listed.

From the beginning, it was suggested that I journal about my prayer time and this suggestion has made all the difference! Why? Because it allows me to check in with myself by writing what I feel and I can reread what I have written. It also makes me feel better. I get everything off my chest and out of my mind. It makes room for the present day. Don't believe me? Just try it for a few weeks. Don't beat yourself up if you don't do it one day or you don't get to it until right before bed. Just keep at it. You will be so glad you did!

Additionally, just having a journal lying around allows for the opportunity to write down anything that comes to mind, even the mundane. That's what I did. My journal became a resting place for my thoughts, ideas and things to do. The way I have written my entries has changed over time but all the formats have provided insights whenever I looked back.

These are some of the key types of entries.

1. WHAT'S ON MY MIND AND HEART

I start with the current date and then I write down what's on my mind and heart. It's basically a way to spew the script that is running in my head. I write whatever comes to mind. It often consists of things I did the day before or what I expect to happen today, how I am feeling and why, what I dreamt about the night before or the song that was on my heart when I woke up. Sometimes I interpret or try to explain why I had the dream or held that song upon awakening.

I often journal first thing in the morning, but when I can't, I try to fit it in sometime later in the day. Years ago, I only wrote in my journal sporadically, but now I strive to do it every day. Most days I am successful.

It has become a daily practice because I feel that my life is better for it. It can take as much, or as little, time as I have available. Doing it often provides value because it gives me the opportunity to look back over my journey at various intervals: the last week, an entire year ago, or even many years prior.

2. GRATITUDE LISTS

I create lists of things for which I am grateful. For some periods, I have done this daily and other times I have just written gratitude lists on occasion. They are often about objects, people or events from the previous day. At one point, I chose to write about the people I encountered from the day before and specifically wrote why God loves them. More information about this practice is in the book.

3. QUESTION AND ANSWERS TO "GOD, WHAT DO YOU WANT ME TO KNOW?"

Before I finish each journaling session, I write down this question: God, what do you want me to know? Sometimes I hear an answer immediately. Sometimes I wait in silence. Sometimes I hear nothing, and sometimes I am inspired to use a tool. Tools include meditation cards (I especially like the ones with one word on them but more words are fine too), the Bible, a daily devotional, or a spiritual book such as Nan Merrill's Psalms for Praying.[1] If you're not sure what to use, let God guide you. It could be something completely random like a magazine on your coffee table or a book in front of you. Don't pass judgement. For example, if you feel a nudge to open a children's book, or something else you've deemed as irrelevant, do it anyway!

4. INSIGHTS GLEANED FROM DOING VARIOUS SPIRITUAL DISCIPLINES

I write down the insights gained from using one of the many ways I learned to pray (walking meditation, praying with pictures/sight, etc.). Often I practiced the same discipline for a period but sometimes, it was more sporadic. You might also want to seek out a spiritual director. I have had success using the search database with Spiritual Directors International at www.sdiworld.org. If you do, be sure to write about your discussions in your journal.

5. EXERCISES

I don't mean physical exercise here. By exercises, I mean activities suggested by, or that I created for myself, based on books I was reading. Examples include:

A. I wrote my own obituary based on how I hoped to be remembered as per Regina Brett's Lesson 34 from *God is Always Hiring*[2]

B. I wrote about each ten-year period of my life in just three pages utilizing only three word sentences, a method that Abigail Thomas wrote about in her book *What Comes Next and How to Like It: A Memoir*[3].

I feel that God moves me to do these activities which is one of the wonderful outcomes of spiritual journaling. For each of us, the experiences will be unique.

6. MISCELLANY

A. Poems: when I am looking back in old journals, I have become especially inspired when I read old gratitude lists. They have moved me to write poems. I write these poems in whatever is my current active journal. I have included some in this book where they fit the subject matter of the respective chapter. I still get tickled about how it worked out this way, but God has a way of making creative work even better. These and more poems are in the back of this book, too. They are grouped together at the back because I think they could be useful to find shimmer words which are good for walking meditation (instructions for walking meditation are in the back of this book also).

B. Action Items/Intentions/Goals: If I don't want to forget to do something I'll go forward a few pages in my journal to a blank page that I know I'll get to in a couple of days. There I'll write what needs to be done. It might be something with a deadline such as a submission to a magazine or something I've been meaning to do such as schedule a doctor's appointment. The interesting thing is that if I never followed through, eventually when I did a look back I would find it. This would make me pause and consider why I didn't follow through. I could easily consider what was going on at the time because it's all written down.

I also include my intentions and goals. These often come on my heart when I journal because they include my heart's hopes and dreams. Intentions include how I want to behave when I attend an event or a new place or when I am trying a new activity. Goals are what I want to accomplish.

C. Inspirations: Sometimes inspiration on a variety of topics come from daily devotionals. One example is the Henri Nouwen Society at henrinouwen.org. You can sign up to get an email from these types of sites. You may also be interested in my blog site that posts some writing prompts. You may find it at www.cardinaltouch.blogspot.com

D. Themes: I notice and write about themes I see during certain times or spaces in my life. For example, the church I have belonged to for many years has a long-standing tradition of giving out paper stars on the feast of the Epiphany. Each star has one of the gifts of the spirit on it: joy, peace, patience, self-control, kindness, generosity, love, goodness and faithfulness (Galatians 5:22-23). I have also attended a New Year's Retreat there many of the years I have been journaling. At these retreats attendees are provided an opportunity to pick a word for the year. As a result, I will write in my journal things related to this word. For example, if I hear the word spoken or written in other places, I will write down any new meanings for me.

E. My prayers: These are very sporadic and I wish I would write down more of my own prayers. At the moment, I often recite prayers I learned as a child. Maybe this is a call to write down more of my own.

F. Random things: Anything else that comes to mind that doesn't fit in the categories above.

Of course, you may have a completely different type of journaling that already works for you. What I hope is that you glean one or two new ideas that will enhance your journaling practice or influence you to begin a practice of journaling. The most important piece, I think, is to make it a spiritual journaling practice by asking the question, "God, what else do you want me to know?"

To get you practicing this step, you'll find questions at the end of each chapter based on the themes from that chapter. After every question, there is the wrap up question "God, what do you want me to know?"

If your current journaling does not include this piece, it should. I think it's my best advice. It's essentially the essence of this book. The book's creation came about from the day to day living that comes from asking God what else I should know and writing down what came afterward. This day to day living is not easy. In fact, the journey can be very hard at times, but I'd do it again in a heartbeat because I now know for certain that God is with me.

Of course, using the "G word," God, requires some explanation. Basically, for this book, I want to define God by not defining God. Therefore, I do not get bogged down with the term God. I suggest that each of us use the term which feels most comfortable. I use God as a universal term. You may decide that Great Spirit, Allah, Higher Power, Sensibility or something else better suits you. The point is that it is not for me to decide what term other people use. It is only for me to decide which term I use. I use the term God.

CHAPTER 1: CHOKED BY WEEDS

In its simplest description, weeds are plants that we don't want in our garden. Even if it's a beautiful rose bush. If we don't want it, it's a weed.

In a more universal sense, weeds are weeds because they are labeled invasive by local authorities and gardeners. In my neck of the woods, they include such plants as the multi-flora rose, a bush with white flowers; the tree of heaven (Ailanthus altissima), which to me looks like its branches are made of ferns; porcelain berry vine which has berries that resemble the speckled malted-milk-ball candies, and Asian bittersweet. These weeds take root because the growing conditions are ripe for them. Unfortunately, they are aggressive and because of their habits, they wipe out local flora.

Both these descriptions of weeds describe what my career had become. A weed that might be attractive to someone else, but one that I wanted gone. A weed that was invasive and taking over my life. It required meetings and travel, evening and weekend prep, an in-box of emails that was never ending, and goals that were attached to bonuses that could not be ignored.

So, I was well paid. But I had become uninspired by the work in front of me because I yearned for something more. What I wanted most was a less frenetic life.

After over 15 years in what could have been a forty-year career, I was ready for a new one.

It is said that we can do anything for a short period that makes us nervous or is not something we like to do, especially if it is an obligation or important for us to accomplish. By short period, I mean a day or weeks or maybe a few months. But stay in a field for five, ten, twenty, thirty, or forty years? That is much more than an obligation and not life-giving if you dread going to work. Converting it to days, the total is between 1,825 and 14,600 days, way too much drudgery if it's not something you enjoy.

What I've learned through my own experience is that this negatively impacts every dimension of life. For me, I learned that I'd rather have work I love that exhausts me into old age than retire "early" from a job I hated for years and years!

Then I should have just quit, right? Well, that didn't happen, at least not right away.

The problem is that my husband didn't like his career any longer either. We were both in this same boat for several years, being pulled further and further out to sea. I said things like, "Do you want to go first? Go ahead, I will follow you." My husband instead turned it over to me, "When you think we can manage it, you go ahead." Neither one of us moved.

Another problem is that fear has a way of stealing time from us. Fear keeps us in the everyday cadence that our physical bodies know. It's what gets us into our cars, driving the same route, because we know it without thinking. We can do it numb.

As our kids grew they had daycare and then before care and after care with school sandwiched in between. But once they got into middle school they would be coming home to an empty house unless we made other arrangements. Although I don't remember the exact year (I didn't journal then), my guess is that I hoped to leave the working world when my son started middle school, in 2005 and so my desire began when he was much younger. What happened instead is that as the time kept slipping by my answer was always the same: "In three more years I will quit." However, because I always said, "three more years," as time was passing by, the end time never came. For me, time just kept moving forward with no change. As a result, my son started middle school and came home to an empty house. I stayed in my job.

Yes, it was now just a job. It wasn't a career any longer. It was weed-like. It was taking over my life and suffocating the open space that I desired to have in order to create something new and fulfilling.

But to leave without a plan seemed to increase my anxiety. I was also angry that my plan to quit was not met with "just do it" encouragement. Looking back, my sense is that my anxieties and anger were obviously not helpful to my husband. I was constantly talking about wanting to quit work, but never doing.

What happens with desires of the heart, however, is that God wants to fulfill them. And not just for me, but for everyone. For me, my husband, for you and everyone else. So, things happen that seem coincidental, but are they really?

In 2008, I had outpatient surgery. What started as my dermatologist extracting a section of a mole to be biopsied as just routine precaution, turned out to be an in-situ melanoma.

Let me break this down. While melanoma is the deadliest form of skin cancer, in situ melanoma is at the earliest phase. In fact, with cancer staging it is considered phase zero because there has been no invasion to the body. I initially saw it as having minimal impact. It just needed to be quickly removed. Hence the outpatient surgery, and then back to everyday living. At this point, everyday living meant that after surgery I went back to my job.

This would eventually play into my wake-up call. For now, it was just another weed. It was something I didn't want in my life and so I got rid of it. Ironically, melanoma did have a major impact, and grew out of control, it just didn't happen in my body.

Only a few months after my outpatient surgery my sister in-law was diagnosed with end stage melanoma. About 8 months later she died from it. Because of my own melanoma, I had a change of heart which changed my mantra. The mantra of "just three more years" became "I only have one life to live!"

Something in me had shifted drastically and within a month of her death I gave my notice. To this day, I still have this sense of nonbelief. I can't believe I resigned, but, man, am I glad that I did! If I hadn't, I think the weeds would have choked the life out of me. Honestly, when I look back on giving notice, it still makes me a bit nervous. It's like standing at the edge of the Grand Canyon knowing that you did jump once and that an eagle did swoop you up, but you're not quite sure you could do it again. What that probably means is that I will be called to jump again.

THE GREAT EGG, REALLY?!?!

Don't lay on them!
That's already happened.
Don't drop them either!
Unless they're hard,
And you're hungry for one,
Then peel and eat.

Don't eat too many!
Too much cholesterol.
Don't eat the yolk, especially,
Unless you're HDL fortified AND
Your heart is strong.
Then drop and fry!

One likes over-easy,
Another sunny side up.
Soft boiled or hard,
Scrambled and not runny.
Make mine a ham and cheese omelet!
What am I, a short order cook?

Dropping one on the floor
Makes quite a mess!
Better to do it at the super market
Than at home.
"Cry over a dropped carton of eggs,"
There should be such a saying!

So many options:
Vegan, vegetarian, eat everything-ian!

What's a man to do?
At least we don't lay eggs.
Mammals can carry less guilt then, right?
But what about the platypus?

The crux of the matter is,
The outside can't be eaten,
But dip them in dye,
Blow out the contents and paint,
Crumble them for the soil to eat,
The incredible non-edible shell.

What's the conclusion?
Eggs are messy and complicated,
They give us pause.
What a complex object.
Only God could have made them!

CHAPTER QUESTIONS

You'll quickly notice that question B is always the same because the thrust of the book is to involve God on your journey. Sometimes you'll hear an answer immediately. Sometimes you'll feel called to wait in silence. Sometimes you may hear nothing, and will be inspired to use a tool (meditation cards, a daily devotional, the Bible, etc.). If you're not sure what to use, let God guide you.

1. A. What weeds are growing in your life?

    B. What does God want you to know about this (ask directly: God, what do you want me to know?)

A._____

_____

_____

B._____

_____

_____

2. A. What activities are you managing in your life but not enjoying?

B. What does God want you to know about this (ask directly: God, what do you want me to know?)

A._____

_____

_____

B._____

_____

_____

3. A. What are you afraid of?

B. What does God want you to know about this (ask directly: God, what do you want me to know?)

A._____

_____

_____

B._____

_____

_____

4. A. What makes your heart sing?

   B. What does God want you to know about this (ask directly: God, what do you want me to know?)

A._____

_____

_____

B._____

_____

_____

CHAPTER 2: IN THE WILDERNESS

I do not remember what came before. I am about to do a new thing! It is sprouting, do you feel it? I will make my way through the wilderness. - Isaiah 43:18-19.

I gave my notice at work on April 1, 2009. Because my boss was wonderful, I wanted to give a long notice in order to finish a project I had started. As a result, my last day would be June 1, 2009.

During the same period, when I wasn't working, I had begun to play an on-line game with one of my brothers. We played a lot. It provided the necessary distraction as my end date got closer and my anxieties grew.

I was worried because my husband was depressed. Plagued by the deaths of a mother who had suffered from Alzheimer's and the death of his forty-six-year-old sister within eight months of each other, my husband was lost. It probably did not make it any easier on him that I didn't ask for his insights or approval and just announced my resignation plans.

I felt for him, but I wasn't looking back. And even when he left his practice a few months later, I had no regrets about leaving my job. I did have sadness and fear over his resignation. Fear was the overriding emotion.

The thing about fear is that it can hobble you, causing you to sleep by day and walk the floors by night. Fortunately, I had already started meeting with a spiritual director by then and she had a remedy. She suggested mental gratitude lists would rock me back to sleep. What started as a practice of listing ten things I was grateful for, grew to a list of thirty-six. The magic of thirty-six is that I almost never made it there; not because I didn't have thirty-six things to be grateful for, but because I relaxed enough that I fell back to sleep before I got there. Mental gratitude lists have a way of clearing the mind of the negative.

The value of my first experience with spiritual direction is that I was encouraged to practice different prayer disciplines. These methods included, but were not limited to, such things as Lectio Divina (a prayerful, contemplative reading of scripture), walking meditation and guided meditation. Where the real learning began is that often I asked my Spiritual Director to give me direct guidance and she turned it around, repeatedly suggesting that I ask God. For example, one of my questions was how do I know what is God's will and the answer was that I needed to ask God directly. So I did. This might have been my first time. "God, is this Your will for me?" I asked.

This is how the weeding began. I pulled one weed at a time. The first one was my job. I began to replace this weed with more life-giving activities: that on-line-chat-while-you-play game with my brother, gratitude lists, and meetings with my Spiritual Director. I also explored new career options and decided I would begin massage school in October. Of course, I still had reservations and most of them were fear-based ones. One example: I was fearful that others would look down upon me, moving from a white-collar position to the field of massage.

As God would have it, the right thing kept happening at the right time. Here the right thing was doing walking meditation, needing a word to walk with, and reading Psalm 91 to find a word. This psalm is about being ridiculed for following our path, exactly what I was struggling with! There's also a statement in it about surrendering ourselves to God. As a result, I selected "surrender" as my word to walk with. What I realized is that this was a question I would need to ask myself repeatedly; that is, would I surrender myself to God?

Fortunately, I received many confirmations like this, that God was with me and that I would know what I needed to know when I needed to know it. These moments no longer felt like coincidences and made me feel sure-footed that I was on the right path. As I had more and more of these experiences, that path became more and more clear: I would be fulfilled by the work and by creating a schedule that made me more available to my husband and children.

Another such confirmation came from a daily devotion on September 15. This devotion suggested Ephesians 4: 1-16 as the reading. Parts of it asks that we follow our calling and live a worthy life. This daily devotion came a day after having been frustrated because I felt like my husband wasn't moving quickly enough to find part or full-time work. Being afraid made it very hard for me to keep my mouth shut. It caused me to give directions and directives. I didn't consider that God was there on his path and therefore, that I didn't need to be. Being afraid led me to backslide.

As the next month went on, I became so afraid of not being able to make ends meet that I started to look for temporary work in my former field. How quickly I had forgotten the message that I was to surrender to God! Instead, I stepped on God's toes.

I figured that if I needed to, I could work in my old field and still go to massage school. I would just switch from being a full-time, daytime massage therapy student to a part-time evening student. As a result, I searched for and found a job that I started over school's winter break.

Essentially, in just a very short time, I made a U-turn, and went back in the wrong direction. Taking that HR job meant I dove right back into a role I had been very good at and had given me life earlier, but one that drained me now. If it was confirmation I needed, I got it. This HR work was just not fulfilling to me anymore!

Unfortunately, upon accepting this job, I had given my word to the head-hunter that I would change my class schedule from days to nights so I could work the temporary position. I also confirmed that the two-hour round-trip commute was not a problem even though for the life of me I could not figure out how I would get to my evening classes on time. My only goal at that moment was to fix the income problem.

This put me at one of the lower points in my life. I was so unhappy with myself for taking the job AND for making promises that felt so wrong. It undid the freedom I had felt only 8 months earlier when I had given my notice. This was not worthy of the calling I had received. Where was my patience?

The answers during my prayer time confirmed that I should not have taken this job because I was undoing some of the good outcomes. It is not good when you hear from God, the Divine Mentor, that you're making a mess of things.

I felt awful but knew what I needed to do to make things right. With my tail between my legs, I went back to the headhunter and the employer and said I had made a mistake. I explained that I was going to stay in school after all. The end result is that I knew for certain that my new calling really was on my heart and needed to stay there.

As for the home front, I had stepped onto my husband's path. I was not letting God direct each of us individually in order to preserve our unity. One of the problems was that I sometimes interpreted my husband spending a lot of time by himself as being idle. What I couldn't see is that he was contemplating, just like me!

I've learned since then. Sometimes I get very direct reminders. For example, I was at the gym not too long ago and I overheard a man conversing with a woman making statements like "you always look good" and "you never wear the same thing twice." Then he asked her the question, "Do you do it for your husband?" Her response to that question was an adamant "No! I do it for God first and myself, and if my husband likes it, too, that's a bonus, but it's not a goal of mine."

I feel the same way today. But I didn't always live this way. In fact, I had learned it not all that long ago. Specifically, if I put God first and myself second, everything and everyone else will fall into place in terms of how I am in relationship with everything and everyone else.

Now that I've had time to look back, I can see the signs and symptoms that resulted from not putting God first. For example, back in my early days of receiving spiritual direction, I felt as if a portion of my heart was partially hardened. Now I know the answer: I could not surrender to God because I did not trust God.

The writer of Psalm 26 asks God to cleanse our hearts with the end goal of being childlike. To be childlike means to have no worries; to have no worries means that one trusts the Lord. On October 15, 2009, the commentary of the daily reading from a Word in Season[4] pleads with the reader to trust in God's promises and love. As a result, I posed the following two questions to myself, writing them and my responses down.

Question number one: Do I trust the Lord? The answer was no. I was still questioning the jump into the unknown and wondering how I could ever make things work in the world of self-employment. I cried a lot in 2009. (From massage therapy training I learned that shedding tears is a natural remedy for getting toxins out of our system and helping us feel better). I tried to contain myself by crying only in the shower because I felt that I needed to stop doing it so often in front of my children. What I eventually came to learn is that we can cope with events that bring forth tears by persistently exercising trust in God. It was a shift that came about because I asked for God's help and God kept showing up, as in the examples above. God helped me solve my problems by helping me reframe the way I look at things. In fact, it's one of God's specialties!

Question number two: Do I love God? The answer was probably why my heart was shutting down. I wrote, "I like God. I look forward to prayer, I like knowing God." I also wrote that I needed God's help to change my heart and my desires. At other times, I've also written in my journal about how giving myself to God without reserve is very difficult for me. I feared that I would be called to lose all my material possessions and, while I admired the life of Mother Theresa, I do not want to live under the conditions she lived under in Calcutta!

In 2009, I did some work selecting an image that reflected my life in its current state and a second image that I used to reflect where I wanted to go. For the first I chose an image of invasive plants choking my garden. I picked this image as I felt my life was out of control because I had not tended to me. The second image reframes the first one so that it's similar but transformed. As a result, for where I wanted to go, I picked an image of a well-kept garden that I proactively planted and set up barriers against weeds. This imagery really got me moving. From it I knew I had to make lasting changes.

The biggest lasting change I made is a well-watered prayer life. It provides the natural barrier against "weeds" (getting on someone else's path, having negative, often unsubstantiated thoughts) and allows me to focus on my own path. For example, if I criticize the spending habits of my husband and kids then I invoke worry and I make God's job harder because their purchases may be just what they need to give them life or to learn something from their spending habits. Instead, I can pray about my own spending, my own generosity, and my own needs and God can direct me.

That does not mean that I shouldn't voice my concerns at the proper time and place, but I needed to learn to be kind while doing it and to use a once and done approach. For example, at this time, my husband was dealing with on-going stomach issues. This issue has many simple first-response remedies. One is to exercise. I told him that I don't want to be silent about the issue because I wanted him to be healthy and that I was angry because he had so much more knowledge than I did about health but didn't use it. He agreed that I should not be silent, but I also knew that I should not nag.

2009 left me with the feeling that I had learned so many things which I needed to use to make changes in my heart and in my life. I began to feel less sorrowful with a desire to move forward and not stay stuck. By the beginning of 2010, I was waking up thinking about my new career and healing, myself and others. I realized that it would be helpful to no longer stare at the past but to just occasionally glance back to see from where I'd come. I still had no understanding of how my life would come together but I was not as fearful on most days.

I was also advised by friends not to look too far forward nor to project doom and gloom. Thinking about a life of uncertainty was not in my best interest. If I could just commit to doing what was right for me in the present moment, I could live in the right now and enjoy today. I learned that, over time, God makes our paths clear; until then, we just need to keep at the art of daily living.

The successes I had were due in part to a well-educated, I-work-hard-to-practice-what-I-preach spiritual director. I believe the other reason is that I was now doing the work. I had started to weed the garden of my life, a little at a time. For example, I practiced walking meditation often and focused on words from the Psalms including "surrender," "new life," and "celebrate." This was a time, therefore, when I used the Bible frequently, especially the Book of Psalms. This book is one of my favorites because each Psalm uses images of God's creations to convey messages. I think I was getting the message.

COMFORT

I'm unsettled.

But I notice.

I ask for Help.

It makes all the difference.

CHAPTER QUESTIONS

You'll quickly notice that question B is always the same because the thrust of the book is to involve God on your journey. Sometimes you'll hear an answer immediately. Sometimes you'll feel called to wait in silence. Sometimes you may hear nothing, and will be inspired to use a tool (meditation cards, a daily devotional, the Bible, etc.). If you're not sure what to use, let God guide you.

1. A. Is there a time you remember fondly when you started something new?

   B. What does God want you to know about this (ask directly: God, what do you want me to know?)

   A._____

   _____

   _____

   B._____

   _____

   _____

2. A. What do you do when you're stressed or anxious?

   B. What does God want you to know about this (ask directly: God, what do you want me to know?)

A._____

_____

_____

B._____

_____

_____

3. A. How do you feel when you ask God questions directly?

B. What does God want you to know about this (ask directly: God, what do you want me to know?)

A._____

_____

_____

B._____

_____

_____

4. A. Do you step on paths where you don't belong? Explain your answer.

B. What does God want you to know about this (ask directly: God, what do you want me to know?

A._____

_____

_____

B._____

_____

_____

5. A. In what ways might it help you to create an image of where you are today, where you want to be, or both?

B. What does God want you to know about this (ask directly: God, what do you want me to know?)

A._____

_____

_____

B._____

_____

_____

CHAPTER 3: A FOOL IN A GOOD WAY

My husband and I had a plan from the start of marriage. He would pursue medicine and I would continue to work in Human Resources, mostly in the healthcare arena, until his income level swallowed mine. Unfortunately, while his income level did more than suffice, medicine and healthcare did not prove to be everything we both wanted. It might have worked out differently if we had been born 30 to 50 years before. The primary reason for this is because healthcare is managed drastically different today.

From my perspective, physicians now carry a lot of the responsibility of patient care, with less responsibility on the part of the patient. Also, physician liability insurance has created a system that often makes doctors responsible for everyone in lesser-ranked positions. It even makes them responsible for processes and machinery when it malfunctions. Another monumental problem is the way medical insurance companies make decisions about patient care, taking away the physicians' ability to manage their own patients' care.

As a result, there is no rest for the physician. The mind is always running.

But what happens when the bottom falls out of this original plan that suited me best (I expected to be able to stop working), but not my husband? Of course, the weeds took over, but also the desires of the heart diminished. I became crushed by the heavy weight of my thoughts. "What's the point?" I told myself. "Dreams don't come true anyway."

The result is that I withdrew a bit from the world. I especially isolated myself from old friends. I did not return calls and I slept quite a lot. I recognized all these things as fitting my mood which was one of melancholy.

But here's the thing: If you are to be in love, you need to play the part of the fool. What happens then is that sometimes you believe in your spouse, and they believe in you, even if you are both lost and you don't like each other very much in that moment. The saving grace is that we were exploring the wilderness at the same time, but individually. We each had our own support systems.

In early 2011, almost 18 months after we both quit our jobs, I received the love star during the Epiphany celebration at my church (see the foreword for more information). Love is one of the fruits of the Spirit; the other ones are joy, peace, patience, kindness, gentleness, faithfulness, self-control and generosity.

When I was prayerful about this star of love, I determined that it was a call for me to love unconditionally which means to forgive others and myself our trespasses. It also presented the possibility that I could love my life including the past, present and the unknown.

The Psalms have so much about love in them that I read them often in this year, learning from the repetition that God is Love, that the words "God" and "Love" could be interchangeable. One day I prayed with Psalm 40 which praises <u>God's</u> faithfulness and healing power which I knew could also be rewritten as "<u>Love's</u> faithfulness and healing power."

So, I set goals for myself for 2011 based on my love star. First and foremost, I was to love Love (God) with all my heart, soul and might. Next, I was to keep the kids in focus and shake the routine up a bit by doing things like having dinner as a picnic in the living room instead of eating in the kitchen, taking the kids out for ice cream or some other kid-like activity. Third, Valentine's Day was coming up and I was to focus on all of us, including me. The fourth goal was to focus on my health and the last one was to let Love lead me in all areas of my life.

When I asked God what else I needed to know about these goals, what I heard was that I should consider the words "Love's healing power and loving unconditionally" to mean that I was not to find fault and that I was to let God heal me, my husband and others, that it was not my job. What was my job? To be kind, loving, compassionate and understanding. Apparently, God had a plan for me.

I wasn't sure I wanted to know the details, but over time it became evident that God loved me and my family. This helped me remember that my family is a treasure to me. Regarding my husband, specifically, I remembered that he is the one person who has brought the most joy into my life.

This was a turnaround from where I had been standing. It was a place of "how could he this and how could he that?" From a different vantage point, I thought something new: how could I expect him to continue to be my best friend if I wasn't a best friend to him? At some point, I learned two things that applied. One is that the pill for bitterness is forgiveness. Two, I learned that the meaning given to the name Marie, my name, is bitter. I did not want to stay here.

One of the prayer methods that I had been taught is to pick something insightful to read and then find the phrase that shimmers for you. Once you have made your selection, you break the phrase apart in different ways and contemplate the meaning. At this time, I often used a variety of daily devotionals which recommended a Bible passage for the day. One time the verses were from Micah 7:18-20. What shimmered for me was the phrase "(God) delights to show mercy." When I broke it down I came up with new phrases based on synonyms of these words:

Take joy in loving

Happily forgive

Enjoy being compassionate

When I was young I thought that I would not have any trials or tribulations where marriage was concerned. I thought I would have a perfect life in marriage. Let's face it, we all do, or we would not get married!

But I know now that this is not true. Even as we joyously plan our 25th anniversary trip, I know this isn't true. What I have learned is that sometimes we need to turn our focus away from our spouses in order to heal or grow ourselves. This may or may not lead to a better marriage, but we do it for our own survival, or maybe even in the cases of terminal illness, for our best death. And this is not one-sided. Our significant others will also have such times. Maybe it's a time to deal with past demons or an illness or chronic body ache; maybe it's a time to go within. I had such experiences. And so I asked God to help me, and as a result, I created this simple prayer:

I ask You, God, to let my husband know that my heart is in safe-keeping for him. I also hope that his heart is in safe-keeping for me when I am ready to receive it again. In all these things, I pray in Your Name. Amen.

In *What Comes Next and How to Like It: A Memoir written* by Abigail Thomas she talks about leading writer's workshops and challenging people to write about a ten-year period of their life utilizing only 3 word sentences[5]. I started with the ten-year period that included early marriage and the births of our children.

This is part of that exercise, written in my journal on Thursday Feb. 11, 2016:

It was 1994. Life held promise. Time to go. New jobs anticipated. Moved from hometown. Relocating was exciting. Had baby inside. Everything was unknown. I had him. He had me. We had foundation. We were ready. We each grew.

Thankfully, my husband is still my closest friend. I think he is the most remarkable man I know, probably because I know more of his story than I do the story of anyone else. I don't say best friend here, or that I know all his story, because I can't be or know that, only God can. But I can tell you that I get to see many aspects of his life up close, and from what I can see, God didn't miss a thing. My husband couldn't be in the awesome position that he is in now, teaching students interested in the health sciences, without his former career and life experiences. He gets so many accolades from students that it's evident his heart is singing.

Of course, there are many challenges at the different life stages, with more to come, but at the end of the day we have learned to rest well next to each other. I am so grateful that we each risked being fools then and now. We are fools in a good way.

DAY OFF

We count our blessings
When hubby and I have the day off
And our license-carrying children
Have places to be.

Stuck at home,
We stay in bed all day.
Did you hear me?
We stay in bed ALL DAY!

Until the children come home,
Then quick!
Close the books and mags, put
the dishes in the sink, make
the bed, open
the blinds, put
on day-ware.
Non-cha-lant-ly
Greet the kids.

CHAPTER QUESTIONS

You'll quickly notice that question B is always the same because the thrust of the book is to involve God on your journey. Sometimes you'll hear an answer immediately. Sometimes you'll feel called to wait in silence. Sometimes you may hear nothing, and will be inspired to use a tool (meditation cards, a daily devotional, the Bible, etc.). If you're not sure what to use, let God guide you.

1. A. Are you in love? Why did you give the answer you gave?

   B. What does God want you to know about this (ask directly: God, what do you want me to know?)

A._____

_____

_____

B._____

_____

_____

2. A. How do you feel about your past?

   B. What does God want you to know about this (ask directly: God, what do you want me to know?)

A._____

_____

_____

B._____

_____

_____

3. A. How do you feel about your present?

B. What does God want you to know about this (ask directly: God, what do you want me to know?)

A._____

_____

_____

B._____

_____

_____

4. A. How do you feel about the unknown?

B. What does God want you to know about this (ask directly: God, what do you want me to know?)

A._____

_____

_____

B._____

_____

_____

5. A. Did you look up the meaning of your name yet?

   B. What does God want you to know about this (ask directly: God, what do you want me to know?)

A._____

_____

_____

B._____

_____

_____

6. A. Do you feel called to write a marriage prayer? Why or why not?

   B. What does God want you to know about this (ask directly: God, what do you want me to know?)

A._____

_____

_____

B._____

_____

_____

CHAPTER 4: PLANTING NEW LIFE

When you believe that God is on your path, God begins to show up in everything.

On September 15, 2009, I picked the words "new life" as my shimmer words from one of the Psalms and I did walking meditation with them. I said these words over and over in my head as I walked to Barnes and Noble. When I got there, I looked at the clearance items and saw a box of cards wrapped in cellophane paper. I couldn't open it but I saw that it included a book *called Bird Signs: Guidance and Wisdom from Our Feathered Friends* by G. G. Carbone (2007, New World Library). There were birds all over the packaging and I was just getting more into birding by going on bird walks at the local preserve. It wasn't more than five dollars and everything about them said "buy me!" So I did.

When I got home and opened the package, I could not figure out what I was going to do with them. They were pretty but they were tarot cards and I didn't practice tarot. Each card had one bird on them along with a tarot meaning for that bird. For example, the word on the great blue heron card was "patience." The word on the North American cardinal card was "transformation."

I set them aside because I was starting school and I could not see their application. But it wasn't long before everything clicked in relation to those cards. I decided I was going to name my business Cardinal Touch because the dictionary meaning of the word "cardinal" means essential and I feel that massage is essential to our health. It was a bonus that the cardinal bird card from the box set had the word transformation on it because my new business was part of my transformation.

Eventually it clicked even further. At school, I was taught that you should always give your clients something at the end of the session. As a result, I decided I would let my clients pick one of the bird cards at the end of each massage and explained that the cards had many uses and they could decide what to do with them. I provided some suggestions: the word on them could be the focus word for walking meditation; the card could be a bookmark; they could be inspired to learn more about the world of birds from these cards; or they could pass it on to a friend, or something else of their choosing. What I've learned from my clients is that their choosing has included hanging them on a bulletin board at work or home, keeping them in their purse or car for further consideration, and other uses. I've also come to believe from how they react to their card that the cards hold some special meaning or timely wisdom for each person.

Other things clicked too. God was also showing up in my waking. I often have songs in my head when I wake up in the morning. For example, on September 26, 2009, I woke up with the lyrics from a song I sang in church as a child. The phrase that stuck with me is "living deeply a new life." This is exactly what I wanted.

What seemed to have transpired in this short amount of time is that the figurative weeds had been cut back and measures were being taken to allow for new wanted growth to take root. In addition to all my "clicks", my husband had announced his desires to get more involved in the missions established at our church and to court me again like long ago.

We also broke ground in September on what we had for months been referring to as Terri's Garden. It would be a memorial garden in memory of my husband's sister. The space was once an area that held a playset and had been set with mulch to give our kids a soft landing when they jumped off the swings or slid down the slide. It was originally created by the former homeowners and they had done a wonderful job leveling it and fixing the boundaries with railroad ties. Upon leaving my job, it was at the top of my to-do list. I posted the playset on an internet sale site and it sold very quickly. The purchaser even came and did the disassembly, so before long the space was empty.

My sister-in-law Terri was an avid gardener. About a year or two before the melanoma became known to her, she had moved with her family to Florida. She had wanted to make the move for a while and felt a sense of urgency to get there. Looking back, it makes sense. She had a desire to be in a warmer environment and to discover the joys and challenges of gardening in a new plant hardiness zone. She purchased and transplanted large palm trees on to her property and created the outdoor space to her liking. She had done so back in Pennsylvania too and her perennial garden was a delight for us all.

The anchor plant in our memorial garden was a hydrangea that had been on the sanctuary steps at Terri's memorial service. It now sits in the front right section of this garden, and we can see it easily from the kitchen window. In summers of drought it weeps when it is too dry, signaling that we need to water.

Other plants came from the church garden as well as green-thumbed neighbors and friends. One of the pastors had connected me to the head gardener and she, along with my husband and I, thinned out the church's beds and introduced these plants to the hydrangea. The space was starting to fill in.

On October 5, I began school. My daughter, who was almost eleven at the time, told me to "Be myself and stand out!"

My prayer disciplines during the six months I was in school were the ACTS model and self-guided meditation. These two methods were often done driving on my way to and from school so I did not always write about the experience in my journal. I wish I had.

ACTS is an acronym to help us remember some of the different types of prayer. A simple method for journaling our prayers is to write out the letters on individual lines on any given day and write the respective types of prayers next to them.

A (adoration)

C (confession)

T (thanksgiving)

S (supplication/requests)

Example:

Adoration: God, I am amazed at the capabilities of the human body and the human heart; what magnificent work, my Almighty Creator

Confession: I am sorry that I cannot completely shake the doom and gloom. I do not have complete trust in You

Thanksgiving: Thank you for the extra time with my daughter today, God. She was up early to read and do homework and so was I!

Supplication: Lord, please create in me a clean heart and put a right spirit within

Self-guided meditation is where you mentally lead yourself to a destination that could be real or fabricated. My spiritual director recommended that I sit with the imagery of Jesus and present the questions I had on my heart. I often imagined meeting with Jesus after climbing a metal circular staircase that went up through the clouds. I can't imagine that I told anyone about this practice, because after all, doesn't it sound crazy? It did to me then, and still does a bit now, but more so then because I had a lot of resistance inside me. I said I wanted to wholly feel the Spirit as I did when I was a child, but my resistance to it was still palpable.

By middle of January I said that I was happy, that I felt like I wanted to give the massage career a real try and not put my resume out there for any more HR jobs. My husband's response was "OK". This was after the sermon earlier in the day that had referenced faithfulness. That's when he told me that the name Edward, his name, means "faithful guardian." It was only a few days later that Ed announced that he was going back to school, that he wanted to teach.

It was in this same month that I dreamt of Terri. In the dream, Terri was on a roller coaster having a wonderful time. She splashed water in my face. The two things, water on a rollercoaster, may seem completely unrelated, but in the dream, it had made perfect sense. When I consider it now, I think the dream said, "Enjoy the ride that is your life, Marie."

By now the second semester of massage school was in full swing. Because I had wanted to have a full experience with school (remember my daughter had given me strong advice: "be yourself and stand out Mom!), I applied for one of two spots to travel with the Villanova Swim Team. It would be an unpaid internship for four days in Pittsburgh to provide massage to their students at the state diving and swimming championship. I remember thinking that I had no idea how to take what I had learned in the classroom into the real world. I was extremely uncomfortable at the outset and watched the massage therapists from the other teams at work, asking questions of them while the swimmers competed.

One of these massage therapists who was a little older than me (I was 43), had been in the field for some years and worked independently. Her husband was in the armed forces and was frequently away, so her work provided her with fulfillment and meaningful relationships. She also talked about traveling to different places in the world to obtain her continuing education credits. That stayed with me.

I would be graduating in April so the month of March was a fertile time for thoughts around creating my business. There was always talk in class about the importance of staying in the present while working on clients. I think that must have been on my heart.

As a result, on one of my self-guided imagery meditations I "met" with Jesus in my mind in the nature preserve near my house. What was revealed to me is that I should stay in the zone with clients, like I do when I am snowshoeing, and remember to consecrate each session in order to be fully present. The application is to actively, but silently, recognize that each client is a child of God, and to ask God to help me heal, relax or comfort the client, providing them with what they need. I still do this today.

At the graduation ceremony in April my classmates presented me with the Mary Jo Myers award. In my acceptance speech, I said "God doesn't call the qualified, He qualifies the called," meaning God prepares each person uniquely for the work they are intended to do. This is based on the bible verses 1 Corinthians 1: 27-29 It made me emotional, probably because I walked a fine line between having complete trust in God and thinking I must be insane. After all, my husband was only starting school now so we were still living off reserves and I would only get paid when I had a client in front of me. What I kept hearing, however, is that massage won't be a dead end.

Fortunately, our lives were filled with supportive friends and family. We had lots of fun distractions, visiting family in different states and doing activities locally with our children who were not yet driving and needed chaperones. We had the gift of time.

Time blesses the gardener, too. Terri's Garden had come into bloom and we had glorious weather for the dedication ceremony. Our pastor, who had been so crucial to connecting us with all the right people in our community, was there to do the dedication. Terri's husband was there, too, along with Terri's daughter and Ed's other siblings and families. We also had friends come, many were from the neighborhood and church as well as friends of old.

There were three readings about biblical gardens: Adam being created from clay in the Old Testament, Gethsemane from the Gospel of Luke, and one from Revelation which I don't think I had ever heard and can't remember now because I didn't write it in my journal (oops!).

My husband spoke about what the creation of this garden meant to him and thanked the guests. Each guest then pointed out their plant donations. The combination of plants looked fantastic and no two had given the same thing to the garden. The irises had special meaning because they had come from the house that Terri and Ed and the others had grown up in. Their father had been the gardener there and Loretta, the oldest, was wise enough to dig some up the night before the house sold. The only annuals planted were from Terri's husband. They were pansies, a favorite of hers.

We now consider this garden a community garden because when we thin out the plants we offer them to whomever has space to grow them. These plants are special. They grew as our new life grew.

TERRI'S GARDEN

Come join me in the garden
When coral bells ring

The bluebells had their time
When it was spring

Father was the gardener
Of our home, long ago

He thought we didn't notice
The irises in a row

You remembered the pansies
They provide the right splash

Thank you for planting them
Now off with you, dash

The lamb's ear multiplies
And softens your sorrow

New growth pushes the earth
With hope for tomorrow

Astilbe abounds
Planted by you, just for me

Hydrangeas fill the senses
To smell, to touch, to see

A maple tree as anchor
Hugs you with its shade

Jacob's Ladder for your journey
That for you God has made

I wrote the first version of this poem the day after the ceremony. It's the only one in this book not inspired by a gratitude list, but there is still gratitude in it. I revised it after looking back. I think it's better now.

CHAPTER QUESTIONS

You'll quickly notice that question B is always the same because the thrust of the book is to involve God on your journey. Sometimes you'll hear an answer immediately. Sometimes you'll feel called to wait in silence. Sometimes you may hear nothing, and will be inspired to use a tool (meditation cards, a daily devotional, the Bible, etc.). If you're not sure what to use, let God guide you.

1. A. Do you need to empty out space somewhere in order to make room for something else? Where?

    B. What does God want you to know about this (ask directly: God, what do you want me to know?)

A._____

_____

_____

B._____

_____

_____

2. A. Is there something you've uncovered recently that makes more sense because you looked back?

    B. What does God want you to know about this (ask directly: God, what do you want me to know?)

A._____

_____

_____

B._____

_____

_____

3. A. Are you waking up with any songs in your head? Which ones?

B. What does God want you to know about this (ask directly: God, what do you want me to know?)

A._____

_____

_____

B._____

_____

_____

4. A. Have you already heard of the ACTS model for prayer? What do you think of it?

B. What does God want you to know about this (ask directly: God, what do you want me to know?)

A._____

_____

_____

B._____

_____

_____

5. A. What are you resisting today?

   B. What does God want you to know about this (ask directly: God, what do you want me to know?)

A._____

_____

_____

B._____

_____

_____

6. A. What does your name mean? You may want to consider your first, middle and last name.

   B. What does God want you to know about this (ask directly: God, what do you want me to know?)

A._____

_____

_____

B._____

_____

_____

7. A. How are you staying in the present?

   B. What does God want you to know about this (ask directly: God, what do you want me to know?)

A._____

_____

_____

B._____

_____

_____

CHAPTER 5: SIDE PATHS

Many people, and rightly so, choose to start a new career as an evening or weekend pursuit while they are working full time. It makes sense to do that. I've seen people do this very successfully. They are often motivated because they are almost ready to retire, at which time they will have access to a pension or retirement plan while they continue to create their new life.

I didn't do it that way. I quit my job outright. As a result, I had a lot of time on my hands, especially before and after the six months I was in massage school. Yes, I joined local business organizations that provided networking opportunities. Yes, I stayed in touch with my classmates who were also going into solo practice and shared marketing strategies, which led me to creating the right on-line presence for my business. But I still had time. What a blessing is the gift of time.

I ended up pursuing so many different things, it probably seemed to many people that I was a chicken without a head, going in every direction. At the time, it looked even to me, that the things I was doing did not have any connection. The thing is, I was making decisions based on one very basic desire: I wanted to have an impact on my local community. Influencing the global field was just too daunting for me then. I wanted to make a difference with my own family, in my own neighborhood.

From a business standpoint, I chose my reach to be primarily within 5 miles from which to draw clients to my studio and to do corporate chair massage. When it made sense, I would go farther.

From an interest standpoint, I pursued those things which I got excited about when they came into my field of vision. It is in the looking back that I can see that it put me on the right track. What I now know is that every so often I take a side loop that eventually brings me back to the bigger path. These smaller loops are necessary. Without them I would not have the qualifications or knowledge to pursue the next thing. For example, I am an avid birder and gardener. During my first career, I was already a subscriber to Birds and Blooms Magazine which advocates gardening for the birds, meaning one should landscape and plant native shrubs which attract a variety of native birds. I already mentioned finding those bird cards on clearance. This was part of the loop. With the book that came with the cards, I began learning more about behaviors and other qualities of the various birds, especially those in my own backyard.

Because I had Saturday mornings available until I built up regular Saturday clientele, I went to the local ecological preserve to join the other birders. From there I learned of other local bird walks. And when my Saturdays filled with work, I found bird clubs to join for walks during the week.

Home gardening is also part of this side loop. Together, with my husband, we created an ever-larger vegetable garden year over year. At the same time, we took an interest in the few small perennial gardens which had already existed in our front and back yards. Over time, we dug up more patches of lawn. Now our collective vegetable and perennial gardens are quite extensive, and we can often be found outside in them.

I read something in early 2011 in *Birds and Blooms* about master gardening programs. I had heard about them before, but now was extremely interested. Upon investigating, not only did I find an active one in my county,

I learned that they were interviewing for trainee spots right then and that I needed to submit my application immediately if I was interested. I was interested! So just in the nick of time I applied, interviewed, and was selected for this program which trains volunteers to provide garden advice to the community. It also has a side benefit for the Master Gardener to learn and make friends with other avid gardeners.

The classes wouldn't start until the end of summer and would be held two days each week. I would need to hold those spaces for ten weeks but I could do that because I controlled my calendar and I was flexible, seeing clients days, evenings and Saturdays. In fact, I could never physically see as many clients as I had time or space in my schedule for, because my physical body would not hold up to that.

So, once that commitment to Master Gardener training was made, but was not looming, I could pursue something else until the training began. What came next was a desire to be a more comfortable speaker. Someone told me about a local chapter of Toastmaster's International, and I was off and running. After checking it out I signed up immediately and was assigned an awesome mentor and began giving speeches. I gave nine speeches in a very short amount of time. I did so by grabbing the next available spot at each up-coming meeting. I never gave the tenth speech which fell in the category of motivational speeches. At that time, I didn't think I had anything to talk about. I do now!

Looking back, I would say that the Toastmaster's loop was a small one. I completed it in a short amount of time. It came about pretty early in my journey to create a new life. I use the term small since it didn't take up that much space in time. Nevertheless, it was very impactful because the skills I learned applied to so many aspects of my new life. First, I learned to give a thirty second elevator speech about myself. This helps immensely when you are creating a business. Second, I learned an easy format for speeches. I also learned tactics to calm nerves before a speech such as pumping my hands by my sides. (No one knows I am doing this except me and it really helps). Finally, I learned some tips to communicate better. One is to rephrase what someone else says to confirm understanding. This helps immensely with clients and, as you can imagine, teens. I will always have work to do here, no matter the ages of my family members, because I want these relationships to continue to improve. I do this by learning ways to be a better listener, something that I struggle with.

The master gardener (MG) path, on the other hand, is a much longer loop and came after the speech training. The order makes sense. After all, I would need these skills in the MG program. The training required us to give a speech on a gardening topic of our choice in order to graduate. Also, to maintain my MG title, I need to volunteer a certain number of hours each year. One way I do this is by speaking at garden clubs, schools and other venues about a garden topic of my choosing. I speak about compost-ing because I do this in my own garden. The improvement of my speaking skills gave me the confidence I needed.

Being involved in these two organizations alone has given me great plea-sure AND provided something else. It supports my business because many of the people I met, and meet, become my clients, buy gift certificates for others, and invite me into their businesses to do chair massage.

Once I started to look for patterns, I could easily recognize that I also have had many small loops related to creativity which started from my child-hood. They were small because they didn't really have continuity. But I can see them now as being part of a larger masterpiece.

The first loop relates to artwork. I have always loved art classes and in late elementary school my teacher entered a piece of my artwork into a contest with students from around the greater metropolitan area. I liked my piece and wish I still had it today, or at least a picture of it. It was created using black and white construction paper and it fits with the type of art I find satisfying to make today: art made from pieces of something like decoupage, mosaics, and collagraph prints.

Second, my high school English teacher required us to submit work to a city-wide essay contest and I won second or third place, which one I can't remember (I didn't journal then!). In my adult life, I am always thrilled to get a writing assignment. I wrote articles for the company newsletter in my last HR position. I write client newsletters now. I also write short creative writing pieces and submit them to a variety of magazines.

The third creative loop relates to music. I harbored a desire to learn how to play music since I was a child. Two of my family's neighbors had organs in their homes and I loved the sound and watching them play. My parents bought a small electric keyboard that I played around with. Unfortunately, I did not have the aptitude to learn on my own and the neighbors with the organs weren't instructors. As a result, the desire to play went dormant for a bit.

As a parent, I am thrilled that both my children had opportunities to learn an instrument while in public school. I have been awed and inspired by them. As a result, in 2012 I took my first piano lesson. While I will never be in concert, I can read the notes and fill our house with music!

Now I have an even bigger loop that encompasses these three smaller ones. First the writing: I created a blog for which I do two posts every week. Second, the art: Each one of the posts includes a photograph. The photo is often one that I took in our garden or is a photo of my own artwork, such as mosaic or print pieces. Third, in 2013 my son graduated from high school and pursued music. Taking piano has given me the language to discuss music with him in a way that I would not have been able to do before.

I am so grateful for this path with all the loops. I feel that everyone can have a path that is enriching to them. It's not easy and I don't recommend that anyone take my path simply because there's a unique path for each of us. But I do feel that God wants to walk a path with each of us. There will be challenges, but God will show up.

AWAY FROM WINTER

Away from winter,
my mind is content.
Sun shines on the soil
where my hands hide.

Muscled with dirty nails,
they push away oak leaves,
finding new growth beneath.
Beets are sprouting.
The heart warms.

Bird song all around,
I follow the tunes from shrub to shrub.
Remembering it's time to prune,
I pull on garden gloves.

I spy my family in the yard.
Daughter and husband lost in conversation,
my son comes to tell me of the pig roast yesterday,
created and culminated with his silly adventuresome friends.

Alone again,
I consider my friend
who accepts her shriveled hands
and receives the work of others.

I wonder if her dreams are like mine,
where even in my slumber
the good earth surrounds me?
I'm in the earth fully alive,
peering out to blue skies and billowy clouds.

CHAPTER QUESTIONS

You'll quickly notice that question B is always the same because the thrust of the book is to involve God on your journey. Sometimes you'll hear an answer immediately. Sometimes you'll feel called to wait in silence. Sometimes you may hear nothing, and will be inspired to use a tool (meditation cards, a daily devotional, the Bible, etc.). If you're not sure what to use, let God guide you.

1. A. What's your favorite part of your day?

   B. What does God want you to know about this (ask directly: God, what do you want me to know?)

   A._____

   _____

   _____

   B._____

   _____

   _____

2. A. What do you like to do most in your favorite part of your day?

   B. What does God want you to know about this (ask directly: God, what do you want me to know?)

A._____

_____

_____

B._____

_____

_____

2. A. What interests or hobbies would like more of your time?

B. What does God want you to know about this (ask directly: God, what do you want me to know?)

A._____

_____

_____

B._____

_____

_____

3. A. What loops or side paths can you see in your life?

B. What does God want you to know about this (ask directly: God, what do you want me to know?)

A._____

_____

_____

B._____

_____

_____

CHAPTER 6: GROWING FAITH
IN LIEU OF MONEY

When you don't have an active income source, and you're told to spend money, even knowing it's the right thing to do, actually following through and doing it, is a real act of faith. For example, my spiritual director, who knew my husband and I were out of work, recommended that I go out and buy *Psalms for Praying* by Nan C. Merrill, I hemmed and hawed a bit. I may have even thought, "Who does she, my spiritual director, think she is?" I was afraid and felt I should save money instead of buying a book. During this period, I really had to faithfully spend money on what I considered to be frivolous due to having no active income source. But then I recognized that this woman is a person of faith and so I told myself I can be a woman of faith too. So, what to do? I bought the damn book! That was in 2009.

The truth of the matter is that I have always hemmed and hawed over money. I thought it was one of my best strengths. I could budget like the best of them. I balanced our bank account to the penny every month. If the account was off, I'd spend hours to bring it back into balance. If that didn't work, I'd set it aside and come back to it. I always found my error.

In actuality, while certain aspects are strengths, the same things can be weaknesses. Money holds some of my demons. For example, I deny myself small pleasures, like a $20 purse that would go great with my outfit or is more practical for what I need than the one I have. It might be a better size or have a matching wallet which would be useful since I don't own a wallet. Instead I tell myself that the 2 or 3 purses that I own are enough, that I don't need to spend another $20.

What I've come to learn is that spending money on things allows me to be in community. I am supporting the creators and marketers of these items (after all, someone made that pretty wallet). I am also supporting the cashier at the store by providing the owner with revenue to pay the employees.

The same goes with the service industry. If I support neighborhood service providers over and over, like aestheticians and nail technicians, I am supporting the local community, especially because they in turn support the local community with their spending. They also support me because they get to know me and lift me up during life's everyday challenges. It's always helpful to learn how others find solutions to challenges. What better way to get ideas from others than to share my own challenges at a salon?

Quite often during this time I could not see past my worry, even though I did try to keep a general story on my heart that links to the adage "easy come, easy go." I'd try to remember how some people ride the waves of money surplus and complete bankruptcy, fretting during times of bankruptcy, but also confident that the next success is on its way, and then it shows up. They tell you that the ride is what brings them great pleasure. I would like to be this person. Sometimes I am successful with this thought, but often I am not.

Making ends meet long-term was most often in the forefront of my mind during this time. Thank goodness, I had a new career that I just loved. I was getting better at all the different facets of it: utilizing the right technique, keeping good accounting records, getting out there to market my business.

After I graduated from massage school, I came to really enjoy my new calling. In the beginning when all clients were new, it was stressful, but as

I had repeat business I began to gain the confidence that my hands were healing people. In fact, several clients even referred to me as a healer. My husband, with his medical background, was a huge help in building up my confidence. When I was nervous, especially with new clients (which was often in the beginning), he said repeatedly, "Just do what you do."

Of course, there were some trials and tribulations which kept money in the forefront, and kept me in that liminal space between feeling in the wilderness and feeling grounded on the new path. These were all due to the nature of providing massage for a living.

First, massage is physically demanding and requires a strong healthy body. Whenever I had physical challenges, my go to place, initially, would be "What am I doing in this career?" For example, in June of that year, just two months after I graduated, my hands were really, really hurting me because the muscles in my hands were not used to this type of work and the hours of repetitive motion.

As a comparison, think about going to the gym and lifting weights and being sore the next day and then going back to the gym the next day and the next to do the same routine. The muscle soreness stays with you.

I attributed the onset of this soreness to the quick spike in clients that resulted from taking a part-time job working mornings for a chiropractor's office. The combination of that office and my home studio probably gave me more work than my hands were ready for. Fortunately, my hand muscles became stronger and stronger and the muscle soreness issue eventually subsided.

But not long after, the next physical challenge came. I broke my right arm! It was September 11, 2010, about five months after graduating from massage school. I was devastated. Obviously, I had to stop working at the chiropractor's office and seeing clients in my own studio.

This is the second challenge of providing massage for a living. There is no sick time or vacation time when you work in contracted positions or are self-employed. And if you are not able to work for a long enough period, clients will seek out another therapist.

It was so disappointing. I was just building up a client base for my home studio and seeing some weekly, some biweekly, and some monthly clients. I would have to contact them and tell them that my studio was temporarily closed.

So where did this leave me? When you are in a career where you don't make money if you don't have someone in front of you, where the textbook recommends not working more than twenty hours a week, and it's an industry where there are limited opportunities for good benefits, including thorough health insurance, paid time off and matching retirement programs, you better have faith from the outset or develop faith quickly.

I think that's the reason this type of career has been part of my journey. I had to free myself of some of my old hang-ups with money, and learn to have faith. This led to knowing that I did not need to have an enormous income source, because I had what was important.

What helped me immensely during this time were gratitude lists. I have made these often, both in my head and on paper. Sometimes writing them down doesn't make sense because I am in the car or lying down. I often use them to fall back to sleep at night. Being right handed with a broken right arm made it simple to determine that the mental list was best then, too.

During this specific time, my mental gratitude lists were mostly in the morning before I got out of bed. They helped me to begin my day positively. Instead of going to that place of worry because I could not work, I started my day with thankfulness for the wonderful items, events and people that were in my life the day before. My husband and children made the list every day during this time because I needed their help with everything.

Gratitude lists during times like these helped me recognize that I can't put money before God. Another way to say it is that if we put so much focus on money we will not be putting God first. Mental finances took up a lot of my time. I can't tell you how often, on the way home from my HR job, I did the math in my head of what our debt was and when I could quit that job. I would have been better served by singing or listening to public radio and learning something new. The quality of my life then would have been so much better if I had not worried so much.

Having a broken arm ended up being a positive thing because the only thing I could do was be still and know that other good things would be forthcoming. So, I stopped the active pursuit of clients and waited quietly. In this space of waiting I received massage and Reike from others. I also got an offer to teach an on-line ethics course. Preparation for the course was initially simply reading the materials. By the time I was done preparing, I was able to start providing massage again. I had healed in just five weeks!

When I look back in my journals from this time, I find it interesting that I was reading *The Path: Creating Your Mission Statement for Life and Work* by Laurie Jones. I had read it in 2003 but something had drawn me to it a second time. I didn't write down why I was reading it again, and I don't remember, therefore the connection is probably gone forever. The interesting thing, however, is that this time I did the exercises from the book[6] which begins with creating a vision statement. What I do remember is that the results didn't make any sense to me at the time. I also kind of remember being aggravated by it because it didn't seem to have any practical application. Now, in the looking back, it makes more sense. I wrote:

My vision is to remember, inspire and brighten family values for women. Today I would say women and men.

It makes sense to me now in the work I am doing, especially if I break it up:

1. My mission is to remember. "Remember," of course, has to do with having journaled every day and being able to look back.

2. My mission is to inspire. Inspire is the right word because I hope to show others the way to spiritual journaling. I further want to create an excitement in them to know that they, and everyone else, can create a deeper more personal relationship with God.

3. My mission is to brighten family values. I think God helps us highlight what kind of family relationship we want and helps us work towards this. I think helping brighten family values will be a result of teaching others the practice of spiritual journaling which includes being still.

One of my favorite bible passages is from Matthew 6: 25-27 in which Jesus points to the birds and tells us to be like them because they don't worry about where their next meal will come from. I have five feeders in my yard and, with my husband's help, keep them full. He loves the birds, too, and makes sure that we always have enough suet and different types of seed in storage to attract a variety of birds.

Writing about my husband also reminds me to say something about generosity. In Luke Chapter 12 Jesus warns us about worry and tells us to give generously. When I oversaw the budget, I would decrease giving when money got tight and justified it because I volunteered a lot of my time. My husband gives both time and money, and when money gets tight, he keeps giving it anyway. I love him for that and I learned from him. I began to always give time AND money. Now the challenge has changed: once both people are giving generously, it requires more communication between the couple. That sounds like God at work too!

Of course, when you are learning to think differently there are times when you are not successful at staying with this change. You revert to the old way of thinking. Again, for me, it's worry about money. Would we have enough for x (college, mortgage, retirement, health insurance, etc.)? The thing is, if you're worried about money, there's always something that comes along to worry about.

The next tool that helped me came because of reading *Invisible Heroes: Survivors of Trauma and How They Heal* by Belleruth Naparstek. The book suggests using imagery to retrain our thoughts[7]. I prayed about this and asked God to help me. The result is that during this time I began to recognize when I was perseverating over money and other worries. Recognizing our negative thoughts is the first part of change and it didn't come easily for me. But once I recognized the negative thoughts, it was then that I would use imagery. I would picture God sending angels to surround the house. The more afraid I was the closer they came. I pictured them as giant, full-figured, rhythm-and-blues-singing angels, able to form a tight ring around my house and keep the fears out!

Restless nights were not uncommon during this time. But I gradually slept better and woke up feeling good. At one point, I had an epiphany. Tightwad me was willing to use all our retirement funds, if necessary, to get to the life we wanted to live. With that realization, a weight lifted. I think having faith that all would be fine, even if we had to lose everything first, put God in charge. Said another way, I let go.

A GRATITUDE LIST

My home pleases, in all the seasons -
red, green, orange, blue and brown.
These earth tones ground me,
leading me gently to my dawn walks
along the Pennypack Creek.
It rambles, as my friend and I do the same.
We listen to each other.

Clients come next.
My physical body supports me with strength.

Quick and easy leftovers for lunch.
Fullness plops me on the sofa in my comfy corner.
I sit with a crossword, then drift to sleep,
as my body stretches out while no one watches.
Agreeably paced day.

Footsteps eventually return, house hums.
Dinner of eggs and sausage
connects our morning and evening.
My family communes.

Fading sunlight trickles through the trees.
Night falls early,
sleep comes easily.

CHAPTER QUESTIONS

You'll quickly notice that question B is always the same because the thrust of the book is to involve God on your journey. Sometimes you'll hear an answer immediately. Sometimes you'll feel called to wait in silence. Sometimes you may hear nothing, and will be inspired to use a tool (meditation cards, a daily devotional, the Bible, etc.). If you're not sure what to use, let God guide you.

1. 1. A. What's your relationship with money?

   B. What does God want you to know about this (ask directly: God, what do you want me to know?)

A._____

_____

_____

B._____

_____

_____

2. A. In what ways do you want to change your relationship with money?

   B. What does God want you to know about this (ask directly: God, what do you want me to know?)

A._____

_____

_____

B._____

_____

_____

3. A. Do you think you're worth as much, the same or more to God as God's other creations?

   B. What does God want you to know about this (ask directly: God, what do you want me to know?)

A._____

_____

_____

B._____

_____

_____

4. A. Are you generous? With your time? With your money?

   B. What does God want you to know about this (ask directly: God, what do you want me to know?)

A._____

_____

_____

B._____

_____

_____

CHAPTER 7: GOD IS IN MY EVERYTHING (NOT YOUR GARDEN VARIETY COINCIDENCE)

This is probably the hardest chapter to write because there is just too much material. I can't write about everything! However, I can give you a sense of how God has been at work in my life so that you can get a sense for what I mean and what types of things to look for. The actual ways God shows up will be different for you, because what matters to you, will not be the same as what's important to me. Your habits are not my habits and so on. Here are just a few examples. What they tell me is that God knows me.

Love and Direction in the Library

One of my habits is going to the library often. I've always loved going! I think it's because I have five siblings and my mother got us all started going to the library at an early age to participate in story hour. We also participated in story-time parades sponsored by the library. We dressed as our favorite characters and marched throughout the neighborhood. My picture was in the newspaper for one of those events!

When I was a little older, I won a contest sponsored by the library because of my research skills. I probably discovered the competition because I always meandered when I was there, checking out the bulletin board which listed what was happening there and in the community. I have had a library card in every town I have ever lived. At the library I visit now, I often simply request books on line and run in for that purpose. The new book section is near enough to the circulation desk that if there is a long line for checkout, I peruse the new books until the line recedes. I have found the most appropriate-for-me-right-now books there over the years. It's like God knows when I will be there. As I write this, I can tell you that on one of my recent trips the new book I grabbed was about book publishing.

I even met my husband while working at the college library! We worked for ten hours together every Sunday and began dating a year into my time there.

All this to say that important things happen for me at libraries. They have helped me be in community from an early age. I find good solid advice there, often from books by authors I never knew existed or didn't know they had a new book out.

The Great Outdoors and Gratitude Bloom into Poems

As I write poems from my gratitude lists, I recognize that I can be very descriptive, particularly about naming nature and its glorious complexities. I think God connected the dots for me because I have always loved being outside. My favorite memories from childhood are from being out in the great outdoors: gathering garter snakes from an empty field, finding a tree house there, and visiting it until the tree was razed. Hiding under the porch in an appliance box so that I could read, sleep and play in the coolness is another, as well as going to Girls Scout camps many summers to kayak and ride horses. As a result, much of my adult path includes being outdoors: birding, gardening, hiking and so on.

The spiritual aspect comes into play because I kept asking God for a writing prompt. My thoughts were often that I could write something if I had somewhere to start. This desire blossomed in the looking back at my journals. I eventually came across the period where a lot of my gratitude lists were written down. It was at this time that the inspiration struck and I wrote my first poem, and then another and another and another. And I think they are lovely. My heart sings when I read them because they evoke a joyful feeling.

Knowing the names of the trees, the insects and animals they host, as well as the woody and herbaceous plants in my yard helps me to be a more descriptive writer. As a result, I'm convinced that God was "in" the writing because God is in everything here: the outdoor majesty that led me to my hobbies, and the inspiration to write about it all.

My Home is a Haven for Work and Play

In another life, if there is such a thing, I hope to be a bed and breakfast owner. God knows this about me. In my current life, it shows up by having an inviting home where my husband, children and I, along with guests, come and go. I think it is why so many of my interests are connected to my home.

My massage studio is attached to my home. I greet clients at the door and when they leave, I go back to reading, writing, cleaning, playing piano or whatever else is calling me at the moment.

Backyard birds are what I know best. We fill the feeders and they come, giving us hours of delight each week. During the migratory seasons, we look for migrants that are not the norm for our yard. I simply need to look out of my home's windows.

I have my own grocery "store" because I hate driving to the community one too often. It's our small, but large-for-a-suburban- backyard fruit and vegetable garden. The yield is great because we expanded it until it reached into every sunny spot, including the front yard. I climb out my back-porch window in summer to gather the vegetables. We harvest autumn pumpkins and winter squashes which often last into February. As a result, we have year-round "farm to table" dinners for ourselves and for guests.

God is in My Menu Planning

One of the things I hate, hate, hate to do is weekly menu planning. It goes along with hating to go to the grocery store. Both things are repetitive. I began to notice that God is in this too. There's always a recipe that comes to me at the right time for which I already have the right ingredients. For example, I'll get an emailed newsletter with a recipe that works or see one in a magazine that's lying around. This has eliminated having to plan. I also dislike cooking every single day, but I don't have to because my husband is awesome at it.

God is in My Schedule

It is important to me that I have balance between my availability to my clients and my availability to my family and the community. As a result, I do not move clients once they are scheduled unless it is an emergency. I also don't give a client an appointment during a time I have something else booked, meaning I won't cancel something to see a client. This is because God is in my schedule.

Because of this, I learned to let go of my calendar and it has made all the difference. I no longer fret if I have conflicts. When I get invited to do something I really want to do, but I am already booked, I don't cancel the original booking. Instead I write the other event on my planner next to the original entry, knowing that if it is something that would be good for me, that the first activity will be canceled or changed, and not by me. I leave it to God. I also do the reverse. If there's some event that I feel might be good for me, but I'm not sure or it makes me uncomfortable thinking about it, I look at my schedule, and if it's open, I write it on my schedule and I attend.

To me it is a mystery, but it works. As a result, I have the most livable, life-giving schedule

Coincidences (Cases of Three Pings)

I believe that coincidences are one way God talks to me (and everyone). It happens often. Many people in my life refer to them as "God moments." For me, it's when three separate, but related, things happen that I need to pay attention to and consider what God is saying to me. I call them *cases of three pings*. Here's one example. During one week, I had three unique experiences with injured birds.

The first was on one of my early morning walks with a walking buddy in the preserve near my house. On this day, I spied a cat bird dangling upside down, entangled by a prickly plant. I freed it and it hopped into the underbrush. By the end of that week, all the cat birds that had been in my yard all summer were gone, having migrated. I like to think that the cat bird I freed could join its kin on the journey.

The second encounter was with a goose near the last hole of a golf course. Its comrades were under trees some distance away from the hole, but this one just sat in the middle of the fairway, grazing lazily. I was determined to not go around this "stubborn" goose so I walked right towards it. When it stood, and walked, I immediately noticed that it hobbled, having one injured leg. I felt awful watching it limp towards its flock.

The third was in my backyard. There was a bird I could not readily identify because it

was molting. I expected it to fly off with all the little brown birds which dispersed the second I slid my door open. This one didn't budge, however, and as I walked toward it, it took a few steps forward, always staying just a few feet in front of me. Within a few minutes, it went into the brush and because I was short on time, I just assumed it couldn't fly and went back inside. I still wonder what happened to it.

As soon as this third incident occurred, I knew I had to spend time with it. Why? Because I have learned that if something similar keeps happening, it's time to consider its meaning. What is God trying to tell me? When I wrote in my journal about these three birds, these situations related to some other pieces of my life and boiled down to how I feel after different scenarios; specifically, scenarios of when I do something good, or something foolish or I don't do anything at all.

These handful of examples are just a few of the ways God has been at work in my life. Hopefully you've already recognized some examples in your own life. The actual ways God shows up will be different for you, because what matters to you, will not be the same as what's important to me, but it will be just as beautiful!

I SEE

evidence of once living things
abound in my garden

discolored leaves
have left their life source
twirling to the ground

feathers and fur
lay in clumps
lives taken by hawks

acorns lie open
sapsucker holes line the oak
what a giving tree

I gather all in my pockets
as I put my garden to rest

I accomplish what I set forth to do

before the impending rain
use the last water from the rain barrel
turn it over to dry and then store
fill the bird feeders

move the compost pile
with a pitchfork
plant the fritillary bulbs

empty my pockets

placing items on the anchor stone
which lies at the height of the garden

I feel Your presence
Oh Great Creator
I see Your works

I have no worries
communion with nature instead
in only my backyard

much vaster is creation
outside these garden gates

what is here
is enough for me
I lie myself on the altar stone

CHAPTER QUESTIONS

You'll quickly notice that question B is always the same because the thrust of the book is to involve God on your journey. Sometimes you'll hear an answer immediately. Sometimes you'll feel called to wait in silence. Sometimes you may hear nothing, and will be inspired to use a tool (meditation cards, a daily devotional, the Bible, etc.). If you're not sure what to use, let God guide you.

1. A. Where do you see God in your favorite habits?

   B. What does God want you to know about this (ask directly: God, what do you want me to know?)

A._____

_____

_____

B._____

_____

_____

2. A. Can you think of a case of three pings in your life?

   B. What does God want you to know about this (ask directly: God, what do you want me to know?)

A._____

_____

_____

B._____

_____

_____

3. A. How often do you journal?

   B. What does God want you to know about this (ask directly: God, what do you want me to know?)

A._____

_____

_____

B._____

_____

_____

Perennial beds where lawn once had been

A pumpkin and it's vines spilling out of the vegetable garden

Trees which line the back of the yard, garden beds put in around them

CHAPTER 8: GROWING DESIRES

It's one thing to follow where you're being led due to your long-held interests. It's another to dream big and share those dreams with God. For a time, I didn't see what the point was with having hopes and dreams because they no longer seemed possible. Eventually, however, I began to get God's message that it is important to have hopes and dreams. I was still reading the Psalms often and clued into verses about desires of the heart and enjoying great peace.

One of the things that I began to think about is how I missed getting butterflies in my stomach when I thought of my husband. I think of it as the difference between loving your mate and both loving your mate AND being IN LOVE with them.

During one of my writing moments I prayed for peace among my friends who were in marital strife and when I asked what else God wanted me to know the answer was "Peace be with you, also." Apparently, God was seeing a missing piece too.

One of the things about being married a long time is that sex is convenient and fills a physical need. But it also does so much more. It creates great intimacy.

In 2012, I decided to read *Sabbath* by Wayne Muller as my Lenten discipline, meaning that I would read a chapter a week and consider the practices at the end of each chapter. I don't remember for sure, but it was probably a book recommended during spiritual direction. Whenever I read these types of spiritual books, I get ideas about how to apply the grace-filled practices in my own life.

If you haven't read it, I highly recommend it, especially if you are looking for rest from this often-frenetic world and would like to have God be part of it. This book is a great resource for that because Wayne Muller shares the practices and stories from those who honor the Sabbath and who are from varied faith disciplines. It's amazing how many different ideas or desires were created in me from reading this book.

One thing that Wayne Muller wrote about is what he learned from practitioners of the Talmud, specifically as it relates to lovemaking on the Sabbath for a husband and wife[8]. To me, the required number and specific day of the week (four times on the Sabbath day) is impractical, but beautiful all the same. According to the person interviewed, it becomes more about the intention of making love to their spouses than the act of doing so a specific number of times.

I loved this! I could certainly hold the intention of making love to my husband. But instead of just choosing it to be on the Sabbath, I decided to hold the intention during the 40 days of Lent. As a result, I wore something pretty to bed every night for those 40 days. It did not take many nights for my husband to notice. Once he mentioned it, I explained the intention I was holding. He had a simple response that makes me laugh whenever I think of it. He simply said: "I love Lent!"

The thing about a healthy emotional heart is that it is capable of much activity and desires still more activities. As a result, the healthier my heart got, the more I desired. Not surprisingly, the desires coincided with my interests.

I created a vision board (probably another suggestion from spiritual direction - she sure kept me busy)! The first board (I have done these 4 times as of the printing of this book) has pictures and words from magazines that summarize the types of things I want to do or the type of person I want to be. Some would call it a bucket list but these are not things I want to do before I die, these are things I want to do in order to really live! And I have asked God to help me.

One example is that I would like to bird in other places, some within a couple hours' drive, some that require a cross-country flight, some for which I must travel abroad. After all, there are birds that I can't see on the east coast. For example, only the ruby-throated hummingbird comes to my backyard and there are more than 300 species of hummingbirds in the world!

The thing is, God knows what's on my heart. So, it's not very surprising that ideas for travel to birding hot spots comes at me in different ways. For example, there's a company that offers continuing education classes for massage therapists which are held in the United States and abroad, including destinations such as Texas and Costa Rica, all great for birders. A couple of years ago I joined this company on a cruise to Bermuda and saw birds I had never seen before.

My desire now is to go to Costa Rica, but the courses are offered only during times when my husband is unavailable due to his work schedule. He likes to join me on these birding trips, and since I've made it clear that I don't want to go without him, it will just have to wait. The interesting thing is that now I see trips to Costa Rica advertised in *Birds and Blooms* magazine and they are during times when we will be able to go together. Now we just need the funds to match. Get to it, please, God!

Some would say that these occurrences are simply coincidence, but I think they are more than that. I think that God is at work. I hope God never retires!

ATTRACTION

You make my gratitude list,
And so do I,
On a day when our touch explodes.
So drawn to you,
Am I,
By your laughter and our conversation.
Your love for me, and mine for you,
Seals our pact.
To have and to hold,
On this magnificent planet.
What more could I ask for?

CHAPTER QUESTIONS

You'll quickly notice that question B is always the same because the thrust of the book is to involve God on your journey. Sometimes you'll hear an answer immediately. Sometimes you'll feel called to wait in silence. Sometimes you may hear nothing, and will be inspired to use a tool (meditation cards, a daily devotional, the Bible, etc.). If you're not sure what to use, let God guide you.

1. 1. A. What's one of your desires?

   B. What does God want you to know about this (ask directly: God, what do you want me to know?)

A._____

_____

_____

B._____

_____

_____

2. A. What's another one of your desires?

   B. What does God want you to know about this (ask directly: God, what do you want me to know?)

A._____

_____

_____

B._____

_____

_____

3. A. Do you have a vision board? If no, why not? If yes, how effective was it?

B. What does God want you to know about this (ask directly: God, what do you want me to know?)

A._____

_____

_____

B._____

_____

_____

4. A. In what ways do you honor the Sabbath? Said another way, do you keep a day of rest?

B. What does God want you to know about this (ask directly: God, what do you want me to know?)

A._____

_____

_____

B.

CHAPTER 9: SELF ACTUALIZATION VERSUS SABOTAGE
(How to Keep the Weeds Out)

When I was a freshman in college I took a psychology course that really stimulated me. Some of what I learned has stayed with me, like giving my brain boss the name Nagging Nellie. I also remember some things about the pyramid which illustrated Maslow's hierarchy of needs.

Back then I was so hoping that I would get to the top of that hierarchy in my lifetime. What I remember is that the top is where there's no minding the lower needs of safety and preservation because they have already been attended to and don't need our active focus. It is the area where we realize our full potential.

The thing is, I think maybe I have gotten to the very bottom of that top, sometimes, but only in particular areas; and I don't stay there for very long. Now I certainly don't think I can ever accomplish this; that is, making it to the very top of this chart, accomplished in all areas at the same time. I think it's because I have too many defects and defects are really, really hard to change. And, sometimes, I think I really don't want to change them because they help me isolate myself when I am not in a good place. I can see now that I have used defects to destroy relationships. This has allowed me to not be hurt by relationships because I have removed them before that happens.

It's journaling that has helped me recognize this. With journaling, I can look back and recognize patterns of behavior. Recognition is a good place to start. It's what helps find solutions. I'm sure I have others, but today I am naming three of my defects.

Defect One: Critical of Others

I can be very critical of others. The irony is that many things I criticize in others are really reflections back on me. For example, there was a recruiter who was one of my direct reports long, long ago. They had about thirty more years of service than me. I thought they could be completely nasty to people they interviewed and I really did not want this person as a direct report.

The thing that drove me craziest is that they had religious statues and photos of the Virgin Mary everywhere in their office.

I asked one of my bosses about this contrast between her demeanor and the religious objects. Their response was, "Sometimes the people who go to church are the ones who need it the most."

This stayed with me because it made me recognize that if I am critical of others, maybe I, also, "need God the most."

Defect Two: Pride

Another defect is my pride. I expected to get what I wanted because I was well-grounded and righteous. Instead, my life became difficult. It made me feel "less than" and caused me to not be happy for others. I had a hard time celebrating their joys, belongings and love of life. I could not enjoy what I had either.

This arrogance can also keep me from recognizing that others experience God in their lives in different ways. For example, when I read about a person saying that they saw angels at someone's death bed, I can start out with a skeptical attitude and then I am sorry for that. I often think of myself as a doubting Thomas because I need to see in order to believe. I've gotten better at this, at believing from the outset, but there's still work to do.

Defect Three: Self-pity

Sometimes my attitude isn't great and it leads to self-pity. For example, I have been angry when other people's bad choices impact me and I've carried that from childhood into adulthood. I suppose the part where I was angry was OK, but it gets ugly when I think things like "everyone should have to have trauma or difficult challenges like I did." That's not a place of self-actualization. It doesn't recognize that everyone has their own challenges, all at least as challenging as mine; and some, much more so.

Fortunately, there are cures. These worked for me, but this can't be the entire list because defects have varying remedies. It's just a good place to start.

Cure One: Meditation and Mindfulness

Meditation helps me observe thoughts. In the beginning, I tried to meditate alone but I found group meditation with an instructor worked better. There are so many options these days that I invite you to explore and find what's right for you.

Mindfulness helps me recognize thoughts as negative and even untrue, especially when I think I know what others are thinking or how they feel. How could I even begin to know what is in someone else's mind or heart? Being mindful is such a better space to be in. With the help of mindfulness, I can bring my thoughts back to what I am doing, using my time in a way that gives energy to the current activity, whether it's cooking or baking, praying, exercising, reading, hanging with friends or something else.

What worked for me in the beginning was walking meditation. Eventually I joined a group which meditates together once each week with instruction from someone who has meditated for years. This gave me a foundation that has led to a daily meditation practice.

Cure Two: Ask for Divine Help

What I need to be reminded of frequently is that I should continue to ask God to help me, to tell me what else I should know. God seems to want our request, and our permission. Without it, it seems, God would be circumventing the free will that we hold.

The more success we have with finding our best righteous path, the more we need to ask for God's help. That's because the "other side" notices. Some call it the devil, Satan, evil. I don't really even like to name it because I don't want to give it power. But I just know that it is real and it would like to sabotage you and me on our path to self-actualization. The interference begins as temptations. A tiny little seed that seems, initially, inconsequential, then leads to something awful. Let me give an example.

When I left the corporate world in which I was doing work-related items about twelve hours each day (making lunches, getting kids to daycare or the bus stop, driving to and from work, working in the office, coming home and writing out an action plan, leaving voicemail messages for colleagues at night, working at my laptop until bedtime) these twelve hours became available to me as I waited for clients. That's a lot of idle time! I had to decide what I would do during the day and what I wouldn't. From the outset, I said I would not watch TV during the day and that was a great decision.

Other than that, I didn't make a lot of restrictions or outlines for my days. Not long after I quit my job, I began to experience the temptation to have a glass of wine with lunch. Most days I eat lunch alone and this only happened while I was alone. In and of itself, having a glass of wine with lunch is not a bad thing, but I felt it as a real temptation. It came as a voice that said, "No one is watching." The same thing can be said for over-eating. It is so much easier when no one is watching. The temptation can also be more persistent when you've invited God in. This ugly spirit takes notice and wants a seat at the table. Don't give them a chair.

Cure Three: Gratitude Lists of People and Why God Loves Them

I call these lists 'Pleasing People' because God sees the best in people. God finds people pleasing. Pleasing is an adjective here, not a verb.

Writing these lists really help me with thinking the best of people and letting go of things I have no knowledge of or control over, like other people's thoughts. I think I am so much more fun to be around when I don't get caught up in this activity because I only think the best of people. I am learning to trust this practice and can feel it reshape my heart.

What goes along with the recognition that I have no first-hand knowledge of other people's thoughts then, is that I don't know the why behind their actions either. This means that I should avoid judging them for things like body shape, spending habits and personal styles. The style or content of tattoos, haircuts, dress and so forth are not mine to like or dislike. I bet that God has innumerable reasons about why God likes every aspect of each of us. To recognize God in every person is something we are called to do.

Writing 'Pleasing People' lists only started in the last couple of years. It was the solution to judging others. For a while they were the only gratitude lists I created. I listed everyone I was in contact with the day before and what was pleasing about them (the poem at the end of this chapter is based on a 'Pleasing People' list).

Over time, as with prayer methods, I switch things up. If I tire of one way, another way steps up. It is this way with gratitude lists. As I stated earlier, sometimes they are mental lists, sometimes they are written. Sometimes they are written about the people, places and things from the day before, sometimes they are just about the people. There's no right or wrong here. Just pick one and do it!

As a reminder, these are just three of my defects. I will continue to uncover more as I write down what is in my brain and on my heart. Life is all about learning, about ourselves and the world around us. I have found that there's no better way to learn than to journal, include God, and look back.

ONE DAY

Wicked soundtrack
Plays in my car.
I marvel at the lyrics,
And voices,
The musicians too.

Instead of entering
The concrete maze,
I park in the neighborhood,
Rewarded with free parking,
And better views.

Aster, cardinal flower and columbine
Decorate the pathways.
I spy a garden alcove in quieter space,
Crediting its beauty to ingenuity
And a green thumb.

I nod in reply,
To the courtesy
Of a driver, who waits
To let me cross the street.

The peaceful walk
Glides me to my appointment.
The hospital hums
Providing a backdrop of rhythm.
I feel the efficiency of the lab tech
Who draws my blood with ease.

I must keep my appointments,
But my heart knows,
It must always take me back home.

Today my husband shuffles girls to soccer camp.
Our son shuttles himself to his music lesson.
I open all the windows and doors
As soon as I get home.

Scurrying next,
Out into the garden,
I dream of more perennial beds.
A hummingbird zips before me,
Butterflies galore dot the landscape.

CHAPTER QUESTIONS

You'll quickly notice that question B is always the same because the thrust of the book is to involve God on your journey. Sometimes you'll hear an answer immediately. Sometimes you'll feel called to wait in silence. Sometimes you may hear nothing, and will be inspired to use a tool (meditation cards, a daily devotional, the Bible, etc.). If you're not sure what to use, let God guide you.

1. A. Do you have a name for your brain boss? In not, what do you choose to name it?

   B. What does God want you to know about this (ask directly: God, what do you want me to know?)

A._____

_____

_____

B._____

_____

_____

2. A. Name one of your defects.

   B. What does God want you to know about this (ask directly: God, what do you want me to know?)

A._____

_____

_____

B._____

_____

_____

3. A. Do you ask God for help? Why or why not?

B. What does God want you to know about this (ask directly: God, what do you want me to know?)

A._____

_____

_____

B._____

_____

_____

4. A. What are some of the reasons God loves you?

B. What does God want you to know about this (ask directly: God, what do you want me to know?)

A._____

_____

_____

B._____

_____

_____

CHAPTER 10: REAPING A
SPIRITUAL HARVEST

You can have the life you want. It will be unique to you. You can do it. Don't sit idle. Reap is an action word. It means that outcomes happen after the work is done. *Trust me, it's worth the effort.* The journaling is so helpful along the way. With it, you can look back and determine what you've accomplished and what work still needs to be done.

Remember, too, that you do not have to go it alone. If it feels right, get a spiritual director or another professional who can help identify and remove the obstacles in your path. Go to the library or a book store to the spiritual self- help section and find what's speaking most to you. Check it out, buy it; or, if you can't afford it, go every week to the bookstore and read a chapter.

Most importantly, notice what you are drawn to as you seek to develop a more personal relationship with God. Be sure to ask God directly, "God, what do You want me to know?" or some other similar question that God puts on your heart.

If you don't have a journal, go get one. I buy the ones that are on sale at the local bookstore. The journal doesn't have to be anything fancy. Can't afford one or don't think you can? Use computer paper. Don't have computer paper? Write on sticky notes or on the backs of bank deposit slips or any paper you can get your hands on. Date them, staple them together, keep them in order. Every so often look back. You'll know how often is right for you. It will start as a sprout: just a few pages but then it will grow.

I committed to a journaling practice in 2009. In the beginning, I wrote on average about once each week so I might have one or two journals for those years. Some years it's almost every day that I have written. I have four or five journals for each of those years. Without them, this book would not have been possible. More importantly, journaling, asking God what else I should know, and looking back has proven that I am on the right path for me.

My life matches what I wrote in a February 2011 journal entry of what a good life would look like:

1. Time for prayer, reflection, creativity, lovemaking, family, friends and nature

2. Eating healthy, tasty food

3. Music

4. Stimulating Conversation

5. Work that is fulfilling and helpful to others

6. Money to support myself and to give generously

I am now in a season of spiritual harvest. The weeding of my life, then sowing seeds based on my interests, has led to the life I wanted. My days have such a beautiful cadence to them. I like to think I have returned to simpler days, days of old, of thirty years before my time: days in the garden, days of delicious meals with my family and friends, a community business that allows for clients to walk to me or drive short distances to receive healing touch. I take walks in the local nature preserve with friends and with my love. I make short drives to the nail or hair salon, local restaurants, and winter farmer's markets. I think I have come back to my senses. Thank you, God!

RISE DOWN

The call to rise
Is stalled by the gray clouds
Which hold me in place

The laze of Sunday
Lasts even longer
When it's raining

I get up to sit back down
Greeting my spot on the sofa -
It hugs me back

I've asked for a simpler life
It's come

A recipe in a magazine
Sounds delish -
All the ingredients are on hand
Dinner is planned

The magazine was first
But now I curl around a book
About bird behaviors
Thankful for the keen eyes
Of its author

My eyes break from the page
Because my phone rings -
I assume an even more relaxed posture

I cross my legs on the coffee table
Anxious to hear about the space
Between the last call and today

CHAPTER QUESTIONS

You'll quickly notice that question B is always the same because the thrust of the book is to involve God on your journey. Sometimes you'll hear an answer immediately. Sometimes you'll feel called to wait in silence. Sometimes you may hear nothing, and will be inspired to use a tool (meditation cards, a daily devotional, the Bible, etc.). If you're not sure what to use, let God guide you.

1. A. In what ways is your work fulfilling? In what ways is it not?

   B. What does God want you to know about this (ask directly: God, what do you want me to know?)

A._____

_____

_____

B._____

_____

_____

2. A. What does a good life look like to you?

   B. What does God want you to know about this (ask directly: God, what do you want me to know?)

A._____

_____

_____

B._____

_____

_____

3. A. How often are you journaling?

   B. What does God want you to know about this (ask directly: God, what do you want me to know?)

A._____

_____

_____

B._____

_____

_____

4. A. Do you feel God in your life?

   B. What does God want you to know about this (ask directly: God, what do you want me to know?)

A._____

_____

_____

B._____

_____

_____

ACKNOWLEDGEMENTS

First and foremost, I thank God for healing my heart, being in my every day and providing divine inspiration for my writing.

To the authors and spiritual directors who share their stories and time to help develop others' faith journeys. I especially thank Reverend Mary Laymon who taught me many ways to pray, many of which I still use today.

For my parents and siblings who have long supported each of our own individual explorations of spirituality, and our own searches to land in a better place, accepting varied religious denominations and faith practices. I also recognize that my parents gave us a good start in life, helping us make deep roots in our local community, but then giving us the freedom to let our seeds catch the wind and take us where we were supposed to go.

For my husband, about whom I had said I'd follow to Luna many moons ago, I thank you for loving me and accompanying me on this earth walk. I also thank my children and friends who have supported me in this endeavor. With all of you behind me, my journey has been that much easier and much more enjoyable.

I also thank the Glimmer Girls of the Saturday morning breakfast club, who allowed me to soak in their wisdom and read my poems aloud and give me feedback. Additionally, I wish to give special thanks to Angela di Gualco who came to me through a series of God moments and has the most amazing combination of life coaching, technical, and editing skills.

My book is so much better than I ever dreamt it could be! Thanks to all!

CITATIONS

1 <u>Psalms for Praying</u>, author Nan C. Merrill, copyright 1996; The Continuum International Publishing Group Inc. 2006

2 <u>God is Always Hiring</u>, author Regina Brett, Grand Central Publishing Hachette Book Group 2015, page 180

3 <u>What Comes Next and How to Like It: A Memoir</u>, author Abigail Thomas, 2015, page 36, First Scribner trade paperback edition, 2016

4 <u>A Word in Season</u>, Regular Print Edition, publishing ministry of the Evangelical Lutheran Church in America, October 15, 2009 entry

5 <u>What Comes Next and How to Like It: A Memoir</u>, author Abigail Thomas, 2015, page 36, First Scribner trade paperback edition, 2016

6 <u>The Path: Creating Your Mission Statement for Work and for Life</u>, author Laurie Beth Jones, September 2000, Chapter Creating the Vision Statement, page 71

7 <u>Invisible Heroes: Survivors of Trauma and How They Heal</u> by Belleruth Naparstek, Bantam, 2005

8 <u>Sabbath: Finding Rest, Renewal, and Delight in our Busy Lives</u>, author Wayne Muller, Bantam trade paperback edition, September 2000, page 31

POEMS

These are some of the poems that I have written. Each one was inspired by one of the gratitude lists written in my journals over the years. They are a good source for shimmer words to use for walking meditation. The instructions for walking meditation can be found in the back of the book.

A GRATITUDE LIST

My home pleases, in all the seasons -
red, green, orange, blue and brown.
These earth tones ground me,
leading me gently to my dawn walks
along the Pennypack Creek.
It rambles, as my friend and I do the same.
We listen to each other.

Clients come next.
My physical body supports me with strength.

Quick and easy leftovers for lunch.
Fullness plops me on the sofa in my comfy corner.
I sit with a crossword, then drift to sleep,
as my body stretches out while no one watches.
Agreeably paced day.

Footsteps eventually return, house hums.
Dinner of eggs and sausage
connects our morning and evening.
My family communes.

Fading sunlight trickles through the trees.
Night falls early,
sleep comes easily.

COMFORT

I'm unsettled.

But I notice.

I ask for help.

It makes all the difference.

GLIMMER GIRLS

Sparkling eyes
Because they care

About themselves
Looking great, trying hard

About others
Making meals, sharing fears

Committed to Saturday breakfast
At local bakery cafe

Fills them up
Until they sparkle

Laughter abounds
Patrons notice

Energy is good
Even when tears fall

Coffee calls them
But community cements

Some come earlier than others
All feel pull to stay

Now a tradition
Thanks to its founders

THE GIVING POND

Without *it,*
I wouldn't kayak solo.
I couldn't find my way.

Neither the turtles basking on logs,
Nor the green and blue herons,
If silently perched, as they prefer,
Would catch my attention.

Without *it,*
My hands gliding along the water
Would splash,
Making me blink,
But not seem wet or cold.

Without *it,*
The begging fish crow youngsters
Would not seem raucous to me.
I might not even know to look for them.

Without *it,*
The liquid hand soap
Would only look yellow,
Not lemony.

Without *it,*
The egg salad sandwich,
My friend packed,
On multi grain bread with pepitas,
Would not receive the deserved compliments,
Nourishment would be its only benefit.

I SEE

evidence of once living things
abound in my garden

discolored leaves
have left their life source
twirling to the ground

feathers and fur
lay in clumps
lives taken by hawks

acorns lie open
sapsucker holes line the oak
what a giving tree

I gather all in my pockets
as I put my garden to rest

I accomplish what I set forth to do

before the impending rain
use the last water from the rain barrel
turn it over to dry and then store
fill the bird feeders

move the compost pile
with a pitchfork
plant the fritillary bulbs

empty my pockets
placing items on the anchor stone
which lies at the height of the garden

I feel Your Presence
Oh Great Creator
I see Your works

I have no worries
communion with nature instead
in only my backyard

much vaster is creation
outside these garden gates

what is here
is enough for me
I lie myself on the altar stone

THE GREAT EGG, REALLY

Don't lay on them!
That's already happened.
Don't drop them either!
Unless they're hard,
And you're hungry for one,
Then peel and eat.

Don't eat too many!
Too much cholesterol.
Don't eat the yolk, especially,
Unless you're HDL fortified AND
Your heart is strong.
Then drop and fry!

One likes over-easy,
Another sunny side up.
Soft boiled or hard,
Scrambled and not runny.
Make mine a ham and cheese omelet!
What am I, a short order cook?

Dropping one on the floor
Makes quite a mess!
Better to do it at the super market
Than at home.
"Cry over a dropped carton of eggs,"
There should be such a saying!

So many options:
Vegan, vegetarian, eat everything-ian!
What's a man to do?

At least we don't lay eggs.
Mammals can carry less guilt then, right?
But what about the platypus?

The crux of the matter is,
The outside can't be eaten,
But dip them in dye,
Blow out the contents and paint,
Crumble them for the soil to eat,
The incredible non-edible shell.

What's the conclusion?
Eggs are messy and complicated,
They give us pause.
What a complex object.
Only God could have made them!

WEEKEND THANKS

My sleep was interrupted
By laughter and noise
Of the slumber-party teens

Thankfully, sleep returns
AND I wake to another day

Blessed with a bike rack and friends,
We drive to the
River canal path starting point.
It's almost washed out by recent flooding,
But we stay the course;
Trail only treacherous there

No one was hurt,
Another thanksgiving

Praise music is still in my head;
I appreciate pastor's words
And the time for reflection,
As I pedal along the river

With money for lunch
We dismount and gather.
Good food and conversation await
At Frenchtown cafe

With food in our bellies,
And lightness of heart,
We make the return trip

ATTRACTION

You make my gratitude list,
And so do I,
On a day when our touch explodes.
So drawn to you,
Am I,
By your laughter and our conversation.
Your love for me, and mine for you,
Seals our pact.
To have and to hold,
On this magnificent planet.
What more could I ask for?

GROUNDED

Clouds are beautiful,
Filled with rain or not.
Our fears are real,
But shared, they diminish.
Peace comes.
We have running water,
A gym membership, and
A garden of fresh ingredients
For cold summer soup.
I'm tired, I nap.
Client comes, I work.
My feet are in community.

THE STORYTELLER

The rain delights
The plants it reaches
Especially when they're dry

I could use an umbrella
If I wanted
Or let it wash over
me

It is June
So warm enough
To get soaking
wet

The drizzle feels me lightly
I cannot touch you though
Your "another day" is gone

I will have to wait for the sun
Just remembering your storytelling
While I walk

I WONDER

As the snow melts,
I see the green grass again.
I recognize how losses create appreciation.

My aging body
Gives rise to these thoughts often.
Outside I walk, I do not run.
Inside I turn the radio up
And wear an extra sweater.

I wonder,
Did I give praise
For the tree outside my window
Before it died?
Or only after
We chopped it down?

I like to think I did.
Just as I fondly think
Of our shared moments
Whenever I see your widow.
My husband held you so dear.

From old gratitude lists
I remember the times
We shared an invitational meal,
Your love at your side.
Last meal pasta primavera
Loaded with roasted vegetables;
Hot bread with butter
Salted our tongues.

That was then.

This is now.

No tree shades the path outside my window.

I see the birds,

But need binoculars to identify them.

The dirty dishes have been washed and dried

Thousands of times since that meal.

I do recognize that time is not mine to hold,

But memories still pierce the heart.

Today is new gratitude,

Intermingled with some old.

My love and I still hold hands,

His warmth caresses.

Our minds are still sought after

For ideas and conversation,

Our sense of humor still intact.

When we stop laughing, who will notice?

ROCKED BY THE STORM

Hurricane moves up the coast and inward,
Schools are closed for the day.
We're prepared to withdraw.

In a corner cove
I caress the keyboard
Our son bought from a flea market years ago.
My turn to reach for the notes.

Our daughter sprawls on her bed.
Music plays through earbuds,
The storm out of her mind.

Rhythmic snoring in the living room,
Newspaper on the floor.
Hardworking man lets down
While he can.

To shower or not,
Is the question.
No need to wake up fully -
Water stays in the holding tank.

We gently move about,
Cradled from the storm.
Interactions happen and don't.

These respites from each other,
With each other,
Provide what's needed.

SIGNS OF THE TIME

Trees dusted white
And still standing.
Winds blow gently outside.
Blazing blue-red flames in the fireplace
Slice through cut wood
From felled tree in our backyard.
I sit alone.

Community children visit rarely anymore.
Houses sit empty during the week.
Neighbor's garages release them in the morning
And swallow them up on their return.

I long for childhood days,
In and out of neighbor's homes.
A fireman's family on our left,
Policemen homes on our right and over the alley.
Across the street the milkman's daughter was my best friend.

BORN ANEW

We carry
Trash day treasures
Back home with us
Laughing about extra weight
Improving our walking regimen

Stools will be refurbished by decoupage
Wash baskets will go to college
Other items put on shelves or they are the shelves
All will have new surroundings
And be kept intact

We are like vultures
In a good way
Sorting through trash
We move where the winds take us
We recycle

The trash is nourishment
For our creative souls
We are reborn

SACRED TOUCH

Oh
Holy Spirit
Give my hands
What is needed
To relax and repair
Each unique creation
Before me

A gift to the provider
To the recipient too
May my hands
Be worthy
Of healing touch

Oh
Holy Spirit
Give them warmth
To reassure and restore
The aches and pains
Of everyone touched

AWAY FROM WINTER

Away from winter,
my mind is content.
Sun shines on the soil
where my hands hide.

Muscled with dirty nails,
they push away oak leaves,
finding new growth beneath.
Beets are sprouting.
The heart warms.

Bird song all around,
I follow the tunes from shrub to shrub.
Remembering it's time to prune,
I pull on garden gloves.

I spy my family in the yard.
Daughter and husband lost in conversation,
my son comes to tell me of the pig roast yesterday,
created and culminated with his silly adventuresome friends.

Alone again,
I consider my friend
who accepts her shriveled hands
and receives the work of others.

I wonder if her dreams are like mine,
where even in my slumber
the good earth surrounds me?
I'm in the earth fully alive,
peering out to blue skies and billowy clouds.

DAY OFF

We count our blessings
When hubby and I have the day off
And our license-carrying children
Have places to be.

Stuck at home,
We stay in bed all day.
Did you hear me?
We stay in bed ALL DAY!

Until the children come home,
Then quick!
Close the books and mags, put
the dishes in the sink, make
the bed, open
the blinds, put
on day-ware.
Non-cha-lant-ly
Greet the kids.

THE WRITING STUDIO

With each child's birthday,
I think back to the actual birth.
Each scene is different, both memorable.
We tell these stories often.
Now it's their stories I hold.
Pride in a paycheck,
Perseverance in a practice room.
I look forward to their homecomings.
In the meantime,
I've turned a bedroom
Into my writing studio.
The sunshine warms my back.
I praise the Great Spirit
As I write the words.
The silence well
Is filled with creativity.

ONE DAY

Wicked soundtrack
Plays in my car.
I marvel at the lyrics,
And voices,
The musicians too.

Instead of entering
The concrete maze,
I park in the neighborhood,
Rewarded with free parking,
And better views.

Aster, cardinal flower and columbine
Decorate the pathways.
I spy a garden alcove in quieter space,
Crediting its beauty to ingenuity
And a green thumb.

I nod in reply,
To the courtesy
Of a driver, who waits
To let me cross the street.

The peaceful walk
Glides me to my appointment.
The hospital hums
Providing a backdrop of rhythm.
I feel the efficiency of the lab tech
Who draws my blood with ease.

I must keep my appointments,
But my heart knows,
It must always take me back home.

Today my husband shuffles girls to soccer camp.
Our son shuttles himself to his music lesson.
I open all the windows and doors
As soon as I get home.

Scurrying next,
Out into the garden,
I dream of more perennial beds.
A hummingbird zips before me,
Butterflies galore dot the landscape.

RISE DOWN

The call to rise
Is stalled by the gray clouds
Which hold me in place

The laze of Sunday
Lasts even longer
When it's raining

I get up to sit back down
Greeting my spot on the sofa
It hugs me back.

I've asked for a simpler life
It's come

A recipe in a magazine
Sounds delish
All the ingredients are on hand
Dinner is planned

The magazine was first
But now I curl around a book
About bird behaviors
Thankful for the keen eyes
Of its author

My eyes break from the page
Because my phone rings
I assume an even more relaxed posture

Crossing my legs on the coffee table
Anxious to hear about the space
Between the last call and today

FLOW

Lean on Me
Is what I'm practicing

With repetition
It'll give in to me

On the house door
A home blessing plate
Jingles -
My cue to leave the keys

Now in community
I greet a regular
The time is here

I hold them
In my attention
Smoothing out the knots

Upon departing
My eyes follow them outside

Inches of recent rain
Pulled into the soil
By plants
Pushing to flower
Leaves the landscape lush

Moving inward, I sit
To pray, to read, to reflect
Filled, I stand
Often to clean

Washer rocks, dryer hums
Constant cycling of sheets
Due to full complement of clients

Now that the sun has
Mostly made its pass
My daily longing begins

I listen for the garage doors
To ride their tracks
I want mine home

This evening
Flooded fields have canceled
Our daughter's ballgame

I had held this space dear -
My reward is no clients
And everyone at home

We do dishes together -
Found time slows the pace

We reason through some issues
Sign school papers
Laugh often

Eventually my night owl
Tucks me in

This day is recorded
In my journal
Similar days are on my heart
I move into dreamtime

IMAGINATION

The local honey
Laces my smoothie and
creates a thought:
I wonder which flowers I am tasting?

So much happens outside my window,
Time and space of the occurrences a mystery.
Imagination fills in the spaces.

Back in the yard
Bees buzz the Autumn Joys,
For the poplar's tulips
Already left their sky garden
To pepper my perennial beds.

Our squirrel with the white back patch
No longer scavenges under the feeder;
A tasty morsel for the red tail, perhaps?
I prefer to think it on vacation.

The smell of ham bone soup
Turns me away from the window.
I step to the chef,
Curling my arms around him,
Hearing slurps as I do.

The vegetables are from our garden.
Do you think the rabbits watched me harvest them?

So much happens inside these windows, too.
Rain might get the best glimpse

As the drops wash over them.
Do they feel the vibrations and wonder

"Is that the piano or laughter?"
Or does imagination fill in the spaces?

RUSTY

The song of the wood thrush
squeaks like a rusty swing.
It must be Spring,
time to get these old bones outside.

A park sounds good.
One with a slide -
a teeter totter would be even better
'cause it requires two.

Because I walk the long walk
With friends, new and old,
any would do, but I choose you.
You're mine to come home to.

Children might be indignant
as we teeter totter during their turn -
two old farts searching for rhythm.

Thankfully, the children's parents laugh.
Eventually, even the children join the
light-heartedness.

Even so, bored of it most quickly,
the children run to the empty swings,
first wriggling to balance bottoms on the seats,
then pumping hard to reach the skies.

To our delight,
the swings sound like
the song of the wood thrush.
It must be Spring.

FALL BACK IN TIME

I made an attic run today,
to pull sweaters from storage.
Only a few fit in the same space
that held twenty summery tops,
but I dare not call them fat.

I also uncorked Halloween decorations,
which forgave me immediately
for a year's worth of neglect,
because they again get to stretch out
and NOT touch each other.

Now as I flit and flutter with
black cats, witches and candy dishes,
the kitchen is abuzz.

At the chopping board,
my personal chef works on mirepoix.
The knife turns up its nose at me,
because I don't know the term.

Behind him newspaper
lines the kitchen table, pumpkin
guts spewed everywhere.

We are merely spectators now,
to our teen, the confident carver,
but she still doesn't like the
feel of the slimy, stringy sinew.

Eventually I'll be the one,
to separate the seeds from the chaff,
for later roasting.

Before our eyes
three Jack O'Lanterns come to life.
We lift their tops from the table
to put them in place,
twisting until they nestle back in.

Together, we carry them to the front stoop,
where they will stare at the neighbors' trees
and heckle each of them
because their skin will stay orange longer
than do the leaves.

We don't marvel at them long
because the warm house beckons.
The stock pot hums with liquid gold for coming soups.
We happily close the door,
because the season is fresh.

COMING AND GOING

It's the human condition -
Suffering comes
The second we're born

Out of the womb we
Feel the temperature fluctuation -
Immediately swooped from our mothers
Whose heartbeats had been so close

It's necessary to be cleaned
And swaddled, but,
Even the vaccinations this day,
Which keep us safe,
Still hurt

So does growing and changing:
Paddled behinds, skinned knees,
Hurt pride, infatuation, rejection -
For me, "I'm sorry" is hard

I remember refusing one time
After frolicking with siblings

I was the one who threw the bucket
Outside our neighbor's open door -
My brother side stepped just in time
And through the screen, the water went

Mrs. Bee was mad -
I didn't like the upset,
Usually she liked us around

We made her some cookies
But I still had to say the words -
I hated that part

Fortunately the in-between spaces
Held me in place, created memories:
Camping, games, sports, sledding
Friends who took the good and bad -
The time, there it went

Eventually I found him,
This man I love
Who cherishes my good and bad

We still feel right together -
Nothing speeds time faster

When I was pregnant with our first
My dad told me "You're the most
Beautiful woman in the room" -
It was a night of celebration

He knew the night marked a
New beginning for this "son" and me -
Graduation meant progress,
But he also knew he'd miss my heartbeat
When we moved away

Eventually my own children
Filled in the spaces
Held me in place, created memories:
Sports, instruments, igloo making

Friends who took the good and bad -
The time, there it went, so did they

On most days I age gracefully
Because I accept my wrinkles,
Meaning I don't need a mirror
Because I know they're there -
I didn't at first,
My flabby belly either, but
These things have become me
The heating pad and rubber water bottle
Are much more appreciated now,
Than when I received them
As a bridal gift
Sensibility is what the giver intended -
I know that now

We expect wedding bells again
Because time, it goes -
These days will be glorious,
But I will mostly stand by this time

I've recognized that I was once coming,
But now I know I am going

It seemed certain once that
I would live a long life,
Now I'm not so sure -
There's no sadness or hope in this,
Just gratitude,
For having been and being now

I can even be thankful
For the paddled behind, the skinned knees
Hurt pride, infatuation and rejection -
I've learned to say "I'm sorry"
Over and over,
But it still takes me time to get there,
It's my human condition

This is the creation story, isn't it?
The beauty of new and decay,
Thankfulness and mourning,
Delights and struggles -
The comings and goings

MELONCHOLIC

Smell of wet plants
Awash with skunk
Matches my mood

I play solitaire
Over and over
Ignoring chores

I sulk to the tune of
"It's Not My Turn to
Empty the Dishwasher"

Plans to grill
Pineapple and shrimp are
Sure to be spoiled by
Second batch of drops

A walk tomorrow
With birds chirping and
Creek edges glistening
From rain's massage and
Receding waters
Will erase this mood

The tree with the face
Will remind me that
Changing moods
Is part of the human condition
But, today,
I DON'T want to hear about it

You might wonder how this one, Melancholic, came from a gratitude list. Well, I eventually decided that the poems needed a twist, so I wrote it based on what would be the opposite of my gratitude list (example: the gratitude list mentions being helped with chores).

NEW SONG

Three years ago, I
Learned the song of
The white throated sparrow.
It sings for me now.

I hope it can't read my thoughts, though,
Which say I'm grateful, but,
I long for a new song to surprise me,
Or a transient I've never seen.

My dinner companion last evening
Boasted of quail and pheasants in his domain
Which isn't that that far away.
Perhaps they'll venture here,
To see what I look like.

DON'T GO

So many lights on our tree every year,
All colored ones.
Some things you are picky about.

What was unusual, this Christmas Day,
Is that the house was lit up overnight
By lightening mixed with thunder.

It's what got me up at 5am,
To sit among the unopened presents, and
The unlit lit-up tree.

I'll take the usual, with the unusual,
As long as the usual is you with me
On Christmas morning.

VINTAGE TIMES

Our son brought home
A turntable given
To him by a mentor

Its presence is welcome
Because he has vinyl
From his grandparents
Who saved everything

Speakers needed rewiring
His dad could help him there
A small purchase and quick assembly
Led to smooth surround sound

Some Ray Charles draws me into
Closer quarters
By Simon & Garfunkel
We're all hanging out

The youngest rests her head
On my lap
Knowing I will massage
Her scalp

Whenever I laugh
My belly moves her head
Causing her to chuckle too

I ask her if she'll assume
This position in ten years
When I'm 60 and she's 27

It causes laughter from us all
We just can't picture it
But the answer, "probably not,"
Still pangs, even in its
Sensibility

We end the evening with cake
And ice cream

Hopefully birthday celebrations
Will always bring us
Together

INDEX: WAYS TO PRAY, BOOKS AND OTHER RESOURCES

Walking Meditation

Walking meditation is a wonderful, easy way to begin practicing meditation because it's simple and most everyone already knows about walking for good health. All you need are good shoes, a few quick stretches, and a safe place to walk.

Walking meditation is simply adding a meditation practice to your walking. We simply use the experience of walking as our focus. We become mindful of our experience while walking, and work to stay focused on the walking. Here's one way to do it:

1. Before you set out on a healthy walk, pick a word or phrase to meditate with.

You may want to utilize a deck of meditation cards with one word on them and pick one of the cards (examples of words on these types of meditation cards: insight, success, laughter, observation, etc.), a word or phrase from the Psalms or other Bible verse, or a word that keeps "popping up" for you.

Consider your initial thoughts about the word or look up what the word means in the dictionary.

2. Once you are physically prepared for your walk, take a few minutes to mentally prepare. Simply ask your mind to quiet so that you may have the space to meditate. If you are spiritual, you may want to ask God to dwell with you.

3. Now walk with the word for 20minutes (if you don't have much time, try five minutes, or two even; if all you have is the time between the door of the grocery store and your car, try that):

Say the word with your interior voice as you walk. If it's a phrase, say one word per step that you take. For example: Your (step), will (step), be (step), done (step). If it's more than a one syllable word, try breaking each syllable out with each step such as with the word 'joyfulness': joy (step), full (step), ness (step). This will help keep the mind from wandering – trust me, I know!

Repeat the word over and over and walk until you and the word are one and your mind is quiet.

4. Listen to what God wants you to know and experience about this word.

5. When you're finished walking, write down what you have learned and experienced in your journal. Include what you thought about the word from the outset and what you think about the word at the completion of the walk. I find this step to be so very important because you can go back through your journal and look for patterns, ideas, action items, etc.

Lastly, just take that first step. I can almost guarantee you will be so glad you did!

PRAYING WITH YOUR SENSE OF SIGHT

This activity can be done with a picture or out in nature. If you choose to do it with pictures, I recommend that you begin to collect pictures from magazines and journals that are particularly appealing to you. On the day that you want to pray with your sense of sight, spread them all out. Pick one of the pictures that jumps out at you.

Alternatively, if the weather is cooperating, you can go out into a safe place in nature. Either way, as you look at the picture or sit out in nature, reflect on the following questions:

What is the light like?

Is it dark or colorful?

    Are their shadows?

    Does it reflect any movement?

Notice the details in your picture/out in nature:

Are there people in your picture/out in nature? (If yes, are they close or far away? Are they turned toward you or not paying attention to you? Who might the people in the picture represent in your life?

Is there a specific color that jumps out at you? What does the color mean to you?

Is there an object that jumps out at you? What does the object mean to you?

What might these details tell you about where you are in your life?

Consider not having the sense of sight.

    What would be missing if you could not see these things?

If you have been looking back in your journal, what clues or insights does this activity give you about your recent look back?

    Is what you've read 'colorful'? 'Light'? 'Dark'?

What does God want you to know?

If you want to consider the picture to look forward (into the next week, month, year, etc.), what clues or insights does this activity give you about the period you are considering?

Is what you see 'colorful'? 'Light'? 'Dark'?

Is there something God wants you to create for you or others to see?

What is God's vision for you?

Be sure to write about this activity/exercise in your journal. It will provide you with much insight in the looking back.

The ACTS Model

A.C.T.S. is an acronym to help us remember some of the different types of prayer. A simple method for journaling our prayers is to write out the letters on individual lines on any given day and write the respective types of prayers next to them. I usually include all 4 letters, but you could choose to pick just one to focus on for any given day.

A (adoration)

C (confession)

T (thanksgiving)

S (supplication/requests)

Example:

A: God, I am amazed at the capabilities of the human body and the human heart; what magnificent work, my Almighty Creator

C: I am sorry that I cannot completely shake the doom and gloom. I do not have complete trust in You

T: Thank you for the extra time with my daughter today God. She was up so early to read and do homework and so was I!

S: Lord, please create in me a clean heart and put a right spirit within

BOOKS HELPFUL TO ME ON THIS JOURNEY OF JOURNALING AND/OR WRITING THIS BOOK

The Artist's Way, A Spiritual Path to Higher Creativity
Julia Cameron
2002
Publisher: Jeremy P. Tarcher/Putnam

Big Magic: Creative Living Beyond Fear
Elizabeth Gilbert
2015
Publisher: Penguin Publishing

Bird Signs: Guidance and Wisdom from Our Feathered Friends
G.G. Carbone
2007
Publisher: New World Library

God is Always Hiring
Regina Brett
2015
Publisher: Grand Central Publishing

Into the Magic Shop: A Neurosurgeon's Quest to Discover the Mysteries of the Brain and the Secrets of the Heart

James Doty, MD
2016
Publisher: Indie Digital Publishing

Invisible Heroes: Survivors of Trauma and How They Heal
Belleruth Naparstek
2005
Publisher: Bantam

The Path: Creating Your Mission Statement for Work and for Life
Laurie Beth Jones
1998
Publisher: Hyperion

Psalms for Praying
Nan C. Merrill
2006
Publisher: The Continuum International Publishing Company

Sabbath, Finding Rest, Renewal and Delight in Our Busy Lives
Wayne Muller
2000
Publisher: Bantam Books

Walking the Labyrinth, A Place to Pray and Seek God
Travis Scholl
2014
Publisher: InterVarsity Press

A Well-Watered Garden, A Gardener's Guide to Spirituality
Harriet Crosby
1995
Publisher: Thomas Nelson Publishers

What Comes Next and How to Like It: A Memoir
Abigail Thomas
2015
Publisher: Scribner, An Imprint of Simon & Schuster, Inc.

SPIRITUAL RESOURCES

These are the ones that I found helpful. You may find that there are resources that are more local to you. These can be a starting place to explore the types of programs they offer and then to find something similar in your own locale.

Cranaleith Spiritual Center (non-profit)

Silent Retreat
13475 Proctor Road
Philadelphia, PA 19116
215-934-6206

Gloria Dei Church
Annual New Year's Retreat
570 Welsh Road
Huntingdon Valley, PA 19006
215-947-8200

Spiritual Director Locator
Spiritual Directors International
www.sdiinternational.org

Tikkun Farm
7941 Elizabeth St.
Mt. Healthy, OH 45231
215-630-1091
tikkunfarm@gmail.com
www.tikkunfarm.com

ADDITIONAL QUESTIONS

One of the Psalms directs the birds of the air to give praise to God. How do you give praise to God?

What does God want you to know about this? (Ask God directly, "God, what do you want me to know?")

How do you practice good stewardship of the earth?

What does God want you to know about this? (Ask God directly, "God, what do you want me to know?")

What part of your physical body needs healing?

What does God want you to know about this? (Ask God directly, "God, what do you want me to know?)

What kind of mother/father, daughter/son, and brother/sister are you being called to be?

What does God want you to know about this? (Ask God directly, "God, what do you want me to know?)

Pick a poem. What word or words from the poem shimmer for you?

What does God want you to know about this? (Ask God directly, "God, what do you want me to know?)